African Sketchbook

Preface by Graham Greene

Books by the same author: *African Sketchbook*   *Days with Albert Schweitzer*   *Au Pays du Soleil* (with Louise Bégué)

Sketchbook

Text and Drawings by Frederick Franck

Holt, Rinehart and Winston / New York

Library of Congress Catalog Card Number: 61-12644

Designer: Ernst Reichl

82917-0211
Printed in the United States of America

Acknowledgments

Very profound thanks to Medico, Inc., and its executive secretary, Dr. Peter Comanduras, for allowing me a third time to continue my work at the Albert Schweitzer Hospital, and making it possible to give my series of lectures throughout tropical Africa. I should also like to thank the United States Navy for making available educational film material for my lectures; and Pfizer International for entrusting me with two most valuable scientific films. I am also most grateful to the editors of *What's New*, Abbott Laboratories; to the Standard Oil Company (New Jersey); to Chas. Pfizer & Co., Inc.; to the Fogg Art Museum; to Mr. Graham Greene, London; to Mr. Bruce Howe; Mrs. Carter C. Higgins; Mrs. Francis T. Kerman; Mr. and Mrs. John Mark; Mrs. C. Charles Marran; Mr. Chapin Riley; Mrs. Julian S. Rogers; Mrs. Lawrence R. Schumann; each for allowing me to use drawings from their collections.

To my friends Franz Schoenberner and B.J. Chute, whose invaluable suggestions in editing both text and drawings were of the greatest help, I owe a great debt. I also wish to express my deep appreciation to Graham Greene, who for so many years has been in profound rapport with Africa, for honoring this book with his Preface.

It is impossible to mention the many friends in Africa who gave us their hospitality, their time, and sprinklings of their wisdom. But I must mention at least Dr. and Mrs. John Carrol from Bathurst; in Sierra Leone, the Hon. Dr. John Karefa Smart, Mr. John Akar, Dr. Joseph Vincent; in Ghana, Mr. John O'Halloran; in Nigeria, Mr. and Mrs. M. Brampton, Dr. A.B. Fafunwa of Esso West Africa, Mr. Omiji of Enugu, the doctors and matron of the Wesleyan Guild Hospital in Ilesha; in the Congo, Dr. and Mrs. Michel Lechat; in Gabon, so many that I cannot mention them all by name; in Ethiopia, Ato Yawand Wossen Mangasha and our friends at the Gondar Haile Selassie I Public Health College, Dr. Brooks Ryder and Count Bassewitz M.D.; in Khartoum, Professor Taylor of the Kitchener Medical School and Mr. John Kababe.

My wife, Claske, is, of course, in reality the co-author of this book. She was at my side every inch of the way, protected me against the mobs of children who wanted to see me draw, added her observations to mine, and did all the slaving which make an idea into a book without as much as a demonstrative sigh.

—F.F.

Preface / By Graham Greene

How often has it happened to a traveler that he reads an account of a region he knows well, written by a roving newspaper correspondent, and recognizes nothing—nothing at all, not even the café at the corner of the street where for weeks he was accustomed to take the daily aperitif. Even when more imaginative writers give their impressions of a whole city, they are not the same impression that it has made on the man who has lived there longer; it is as if he and they have taken their walks always along different streets, stood by the river at a different hour of the day, and seen the vistas of the park cloaked in a different weather.

This is not what I found when I read Frederick Franck's *African Sketchbook*. Our paths have crossed in several places. I know Dakar, Douala, Nairobi, Bathurst as fleetingly as he; but in Lagos, I have lived and worked three months and in Freetown a year, and I still recognize every detail of his descriptions and his drawings.

Night in Freetown is an "Arabian Night": the hundreds of little stalls of the kola-nut vendors and soft-drink parlors are aglow with small smoking oil lamps. Long-robed figures move in throngs to the rhythm of muted laughter which sometimes swells into shouting or swearing. Next to "Gab's Free and Easy. Coffins in all Sizes," "What profiteth it a man . . . ?" a record shop is giving free concerts. Teen-agers dance their erotic dances in the street. Moslems kneel on the muddy sidewalks and bow eastward, touching the ground with their foreheads. A group of celebrants of a burial come dancing out of a dark side street, beating drums and brandishing acetylene lamps.

The accuracy of feeling with which he describes what I know, gives me complete confidence in his picture of the unfamiliar: Ghana, Ethiopia, the Sudan, and of the new aspects of the familiar (for the wind of change is blowing through every scene in his sketchbook).

It is a great advantage to a traveler if he is not traveling just for the sake of travel, if he has a professional interest in one particular aspect of a country's life. Dr. Franck, as well as being an artist, is a doctor and a dental surgeon, and his profession gives him wider and deeper contacts than are the lot of the usual tourist, who merely exchanges his letters of introduction for personal snapshots of scenes already commemorated on innumerable picture postcards. In this, the average tourist very much resembles the royal family: He will never be allowed to miss the ruins of Zimbabwe or Rhodes's tomb, but he will probably not penetrate to the little museum in Freetown, a former railway station.

There was a medal commemorating the abolition of slavery. It says: "We are all brethren, 1807." I also found an ordinary Bols gin crock, displayed with the legend: "Old German Relic found in alluvial diamond rocks, of unknown date." In a showcase by itself stood an empty little pedestal with the caption: "Model of the largest diamond found in Sierra Leone" and below it on a separate slip: "Stolen from the Museum on August 31, 1958."

Such freshness of choice in drawing and description makes Frederick Franck's occasional generalizations the more worthy of attention.

Africa always has a touch of the comical. It often shocked me in its cruelty and harshness, but even then it was not tragic: there was always some dissonance in the cruelty or the harshness, which made it tragi-comic. The continent itself seems to be bathed in raucous laughter, but, make no mistake, African laughter is not always a sign of amusement. It may become without warning a prelude to violence. For laughter in Africa may also be reaction to bafflement, a defensive tensing of the facial muscles, or an apology. African laughter, African dancing, African clothing, and African sculpture—even African politics—have something in common: the grotesque.

Contents

List of Drawings

African Sketchbook

1 / Aware in Africa

This book is not "illustrated," it is written around the drawings which form its core. For I am no expert on Africa and my knowledge of its politics, geography, or demography is more hole than cheese. But I made contact with Africa, I drew everywhere: on a folding stool in the markets, sitting on a log in the jungle with ants crawling over me, on beaches while chiggers ate themselves into my toes, and from cars and buses where the interested crowds were too dense. Often children were swarming around me blocking my view, or goats nibbled my paper as I sketched.

I marvel again at the enormous difference between drawing and photography. The photo machine with its clever eye, patterned on the human eye, catches life in a frozen instant and gives us the illusion that this is an image of reality. The drawing hand and the eye which informs it cannot catch momentary images; they trace the thing or event through space and time until it disappears from the field of vision. Eye and hand follow the gull from the moment it plunges down on its prey to the moment it alights and continues its flight. The pen unceasingly feels and caresses the bird's form which changes a million times in size and gesture.

The relationships of leaves and branches in a jungle change constantly, even when it is wind-still, for the living eye moves. While drawing I am aware of life in myself and my subject, I am aware that all that lives moves, however imperceptibly. The young goats, the birds on the branch, the wind-blown grasses, even the dying in the hospital wards—all these move. Drawing is the following of this living moment. And where things appear to be dead, like shells and stones, their very structure reveals the congealed movement which formed them, the crumbling movement of their disintegration bathed in the ever changing movement of the light by which the eye perceives them.

And then, in drawing, there is the miracle of participation, absent in photography. The tourist with his camera breezes through a village, quickly snapping pictures, capturing the shadows of people and events in his magic box. People in Africa now have these magic boxes too; they have lost their mystery. Few are the Africans who still believe you steal their soul in the little black and chrome box. They are no longer afraid of it, but they have learned to covet it and they resent the intrusion into their private lives. They resent the stranger who surreptitiously takes their picture while they are at work, or quarreling, or suckling their babies. Not daring to show their resentment, the unpaid, involuntary models disappear behind their doors.

Drawing is different. Everywhere the children are fascinated by this funny white man, who starts to scratch with an ordinary pen on an ordinary blank piece of paper. They crow with delight when they recognize themselves, their goats, their houses.

3

They sense that one cannot draw what one is not intensely involved in. And in the circumstances in which I drew in Africa, with the sun blinding my eyes or baking my neck, only passionate involvement made it possible to draw at all. Not only have I never met hostility while drawing anywhere in the world, but I have made friends, and all I draw becomes mine forever.

It was a revelation to find that every child in Africa recognized what I had drawn; human eyes, totally untrained in art, appear to be able to read those signs of ink on paper, naturally, without effort. I once heard a famous abstract painter say of his work, "I want to see the way a primitive bushman sees, not as concept but as sheer perception." I do not draw concepts either, although my drawings are legible. In drawing, my hand caresses and follows the forms; a child can read the signs, and loves one for one's magic.

I first went to Africa in 1958, when I set up a dental clinic on behalf of Medico at the Hospital of Dr. Albert Schweitzer in Lambaréné, Equatorial Africa. I went there as the double personality I happen to be. In the first place I am an artist and I had arranged with Dr. Schweitzer that I would draw for half of each day in the famous old hospital and devote the other half to dental surgery for anyone who needed it.

While traveling in Africa I learned, that although Africans suffer as much from dental disease as anyone else, there were hardly any dentists on the continent. The doctors who had to deal with dental emergencies usually were not trained for it. When I returned to Lambaréné in 1959, I had made up short courses in Emergency Dental Diagnosis and Treatment for doctors and paramedical personnel. On my way to and from Lambaréné I lectured to medical audiences in Ghana, in the then Belgian Congo, the Gabon Republic, Ethiopia, and the Sudan.

Again in 1960 I made use of my trip to the Schweitzer Hospital in this manner. I lectured and showed medical films in the Gambia, Sierra Leone, Ghana, and in various cities in the Federation of Nigeria. Everywhere I went I was in contact with African doctors and through them with other Africans.

They thought me odd at first, this lecturer who would run off and draw on street corners, this dental surgeon with a medical background who was really an artist and a writer. "How can you do all these things?" they asked. "Don't you get mixed up? What are you in the first place anyway?"

"I really don't know," I replied. "When I am drawing I am nothing but an artist; when I am writing I forget that I draw; and when I am doing or talking dental surgery I am in it completely, until I run off to draw again." So I remained an odd white fish, but perhaps this was all to the good, for I made contacts with people of widely varying interests. The most intimate contact, however, was through my drawing, for each hour of lecturing was compensated for by many hours of drawing. I never felt Africa as strange or exotic. To me it was part of the earth, part of my earth. Stepping from a plane in Ethiopia, in the Sudan, in the Congo, I stepped on grass like our grass, gravel like our gravel; insects squirmed between grains of sand, flowers opened and closed their petals, babies sucked and cried, dogs crawled toward people to beg. There were huge differences also of course, but compared with the similarities I felt them insignificant.

I am sure there is much I misunderstood. My own cultural heritage must often have misled me, made me misinterpret and hate or love in the wrong places. But this I learned: all generalizations about Africa are superficial and false. The differences between Ethiopia and Ghana for instance are tremendous, psychologically, economically, culturally. And the complexities have been compounded by cross-fertilization between tribe and tribe. Besides, all peoples and tribes in some way have been touched by their contact with the cultural values and industrial products of Europe and America. There is not a village in which this is not evident, if only in the shape of a kerosene can or a Coca Cola bottle, a sewing machine or a bicycle.

Populations have been redistributed, as industries and mines and agriculture have sprung up. New social patterns have been woven, and since the beginning of this century a subsistence economy has more and more been replaced by a money economy, and hence dependence on exports and imports. In an infinite number of mutations, social relationships in clan, tribe, and newborn nations have been altered by this new economy and by vastly improved communications. New classes have arisen as a result of imported educational and administrative systems and it has now been radically proven—and not least to the Africans—that people's capacities are not determined by their color, but that through acculturation the son of an illiterate backwoods African can become in one generation an important diplomat, scientist, or artist.

I felt this Africa was a huge organism, both predetermined and unpredictable in its life course; as a process within the life process of the world and never as a thing. For short months I was caught up in this life process.

There are now many profound works available on all the aspects of what was called "dark Africa"—"dark" because of our agelong ignorance of it.

Incompetent to offer diagnoses, prognoses, and generalizations about Black Africa, a living organism of 167 million inhabitants, I noted down what Africa looked and felt like to me.

I seek only to communicate in sketches of line and wash and words those things of which I was personally aware in Africa.

2 / Via Dakar to the Gambia

In Madrid, when I verified my airline ticket, the Air France man had frowned and started looking through his guidebooks. "Bathurst," he mumbled, *"c'est en Australie?"* "No," I said, "in the Gambia." He started looking again. "There is no Bathurst in Cambodia," he came back. Nevertheless I got to Bathurst and by Air France plane too, but I had to interrupt my flight in Dakar for a few days, for Ghana Airways had stopped flying and was trying to do an empire-building job in the Congo.

All an American-made plane needs to make it French is a French crew. The stewardesses lack the standardized smile and the perfect legs, but they are women who know how to make you comfortable. The captain does not start with the statement that he is "so happy to have you aboard," but laconically announces through his loudspeaker: "You are now going to hear a different noise. It just means that we are going to rise another two thousand meters to find more favorable winds." The dinner is not the eternal chicken à la king from aluminum dishes, but an event which makes you forget the 23,000 feet and wonder how exactly they stewed the lettuce or made the *côtelette de veau à la crème.*

The Italian missionary next to me ate with an expression of beatitude on his round face. We had already discovered that we both found take-offs and landings less than exhilarating and that we shared a very fine ear for differences in motor pitch and interest in the continued performance of propellers. Our strong faith and our enjoyment of the dinner kept this mutual curiosity in aeronautics within bounds. He pointed at a *rouleau* of ham in aspic, lifted his eyes to the higher stratosphere and with compressed lips produced an enthusiastic "mmm. . . ."

Outside stretched an endless layer of soft tufts; infinitely far away hung a pale sun, distorted by the window into a luminous yellow egg. The African sky was a blue-white opaline mass of spun sugar, shot through with crimson sequins. In the middle of dinner the plane suddenly shuddered violently, and all the flesh packed inside vibrated with it. It lasted only a few seconds. The sun was now changing to orange and the glassy mass became blood red, purple, violet, and finally dead white. Then the sun began to sink, first quite rapidly, then more and more slowly with such exasperating retardation that it seemed as if with the disappearance of the last rim the whole world would come to an end.

We watched in awe, the missionary and I, unable to swallow our last bite. "It is like the birth of God's universe," he mumbled. "It is like our universe drowning," I answered, still feeling the shudder of the plane in my spine, "and we all drowning with it, *mon Père!* What are we doing here above the clouds anyway, stupidly flying through space, conquering the moon, although we never could learn how to live on earth?"

Franck VII 60
Bathurst Gambia

"Become a modern African! In the new Africa there is a need for Africans who are capable of occupying the positions which modern life demands." So begins an ad for a correspondence course in the newspaper *Paris-Dakar*. The course undertakes to make you "cultured, an African with knowledge, initiative, and will power"; it will give you "self-confidence to overcome your self-doubt." In Dakar I saw more bookshops than in all of Spain and far better ones—bookshops filled with everything from textbooks in engineering to the French classics and the latest Prix Goncourt and Prix Femina. Young Africans were looking at the contents of shop windows like hungry children, pressing their noses against the windows of a bakery. Everyone seemed to read *Paris-Dakar,* which is completely patterned on the Paris boulevard papers and has a fair amount of international news. Other African dailies give absolute precedence to African news, as though the world outside Africa were on a different planet. The paper is less sensational than its Parisian colleagues, and its column of "African Opinions" is educational and even moralistic. There is something touching about the directness with which this newspaper tries to make its readers conscious of their civic duties: "Don't let your children run wild in the streets. The schools cannot give them a sense of values; you, parents, have to do it." Or: "Freedom is all right, but not anarchy. If we refuse to submit to the tyranny of our own laws, we will fall under the tyranny of tyrants. . . . There is more to us, Africans, than dancing and tom-tom. We are human beings and have to realize it. . . . We can only build a united Africa by consultation, not by lording it over one another."

These articles read as though their authors were schoolteachers of immense good will, and probably they are. Schoolteachers are the first intellectuals formed in Africa. Schoolteachers have to teach. With great seriousness they fulfill their task of awakening their fellow citizens in an educational "operation bootstrap." This is a campaign to make young Africa conscious of social responsibility, of self-respect, and to undo the damage caused by the rapid detribalization and urbanization which tore to pieces the fabric of established age-old customs and systems of values. They emphasize the necessity to "overcome self-doubt" by hard thought and hard work.

I had plenty of time to read Dakar newspapers, for I had to wait for a call from Bathurst in the Gambia, barely 200 miles away. But telephones are usually out of order all over Africa. After a day the line was repaired and for ten minutes I listened to something like the noise of the sea in a seashell, interrupted by shouts of "Can you hear me?" and ending with "I'll send a telegram." This is typical of African communications today: one plane a week, a telephone which hardly ever works, and telegrams which never arrive. It is the same along the whole West Coast, even in the larger cities. To call Ibadan (the capital of the Western Region of Nigeria) from Lagos may take half a day— to drive it leisurely takes two hours. It is worse in Central Africa and not much better in East Africa. No one outside the continent understands that you cannot write, wire, or arrive on schedule. Yet how revolutionary it is compared with conditions a generation ago, when a steamer brought the mail once a month to the coast and a launch twice a year to the outposts along the rivers.

Dakar is very French, but it is even more African. At every step the most dogged peddlers in the world attack you, assuming that you want to buy gold-plated wrist watches, Parker pens, sunglasses, machine-made sculptures, or plastic combs by the gross in order to peddle them further yourself. As everywhere in Africa, everybody who has but two bananas to sell is "in

business" from the age of five until death. You place the two bananas or the twenty sunglasses on your head and peddle or you sit down anywhere with your back against a house, in a puddle, or in a heap of refuse, and stick out one arm to obstruct traffic, compelling those who pass either to jump or buy. Here business is not so much a means of earning a living as it is a form of social intercourse. It perpetually leads to fascinating contacts and conversations and is the best antidote against loneliness and seclusion, which is probably what the African dislikes most. If you do sell something it is of course even more wonderful. But if you don't and people just stop and bargain for hours, at any rate you have not lost your day.

In this respect Dakar is not different from the rest of dark Africa, which babbles and chatters and sings and dances from the Sahara to the Zambezi and perhaps farther down. But in places like Dakar and Lagos it all proceeds with ever increasing acceleration and nothing is more fatiguing than a few hours shuffling through these markets, where the senses are bombarded with innumerable stimuli. In the stalls you see amorphous masses of bleeding meats; myriads of gold, silver, and mother-of-pearl fishes; heaps of those most subtle-colored mollusks called "sea beans"; fenced-in, bleating sheep and goats; piles of gaudy-colored plastic shoes; bundled cassava roots, ocher yams, purple radishes, and amoeba-infested lettuces in softest greens—all covered with trillions of rainbow-hued flies which sting your neck and crawl up under your trousers. The streets are thronged with stern and noble-faced Mauretanians in royal, food-stained gowns and turbans full of vermin; with large sailing ships of women in yards of gaudy prints; with multitudes of paralyzed cripples crawling on their calloused hands and knees like animals; with red-fezzed soldiers; with veiled Moslem women in indigo blue and magenta; with doddering old French widows, leaning heavily on their sticks after thirty years of African life. In front of mosques old men sit on the ground, embroidering white Moslem robes with goldlike thread. On the corners fanatic-looking, thin Senegalese sell Chinese propaganda magazines. Hundreds of beggars lift their mutilated limbs and blind eyes to you. Life has different dimensions here and it seems to proliferate not like insects, but like microbes in an agar broth. People seem hardly born individually, but rather to multiply and to die again in waves of innumerable incarnations.

And these mothers! Peachlike and gay, they have their first babies when they are still long-legged children; their breasts, which have hardly had time to bud, are milked in a few years into long triangular teats. Then their flesh begins to heap up on the long strong shafts of bone, to pile up on the slender hips, the vertebrae, and the pelvis into enormous buttocks. Their majestic torsos are wrapped in yards and yards of yellow cotton, sometimes printed with green snakes; around the hips they wear cerulean billows, held together by a magenta sling in which the latest child is tied, its small triangular head bumping contentedly against the mother's back.

The women sail forth along the streets, their vibrating headties surmounted by enamel basins full of mangoes, bottles, and fishtails. Often they wear over all their gaudy finery a transparent chemise of pink tulle, which makes them even more splendid and redoubtable. Some have in tow goats, whose kids try to suck as they run. But the women of Dakar are not yet satisfied with their splendor; they still have to put on silver anklets, heavy as slave irons, and tinkling bracelets, with seven to ten rings dangling from the pierced rims of each ear. The gauze surplices seem to be a throwback to eighteenth-century French court dress which survived only in this part of Africa, where the French influence was especially strong.

The African intellectuals here had to go through schooling as severe and conservative as that of the French lycées. Nothing was spared them. Their politicians were trained in French parliamentary procedure as députés in the French Parliament and their speeches are still given in the proudest classical French. Leopold Sédar Senghor, former President of the Federation of Mali, is a renowned French poet, although at the same time he is the apostle of "Négritude," the African personality, proclaiming the basic spiritual unity of Negroes all over the world, a unity based on being instead of having. Yet their French culture is the great pride of the intelligentsia, independence or not.

No, the days I had to wait in Dakar were no loss, except financially. For with Abidjan, the capital of the Ivory Coast, Dakar probably shares the distinction of being one of the most expensive places on earth. You get for your dollar only half as many francs as in metropolitan France and the hotels are three times as expensive. Still, the Grand Hotel N'gor, for example, is worth it. It is a huge semicircle, nine stories high, looking out over terraced gardens which descend to an ideal beach, and there one can sort out one's impressions under tepid water after a day of walking the overcrowded streets in the infernal heat of Dakar.

After a week I finally secured a seat in the little plane to Bathurst, capital of the Gambia. It dropped me at a cozy English airport, called Yundum. The radio at Yundum was giving the news: the Federation of Mali had just fallen apart and in classical French speeches the ministers of the Sudan Republic and Senegal were accusing each other of treason.

The airport of the Gambia is as English and Victorian as the waiting room for the ferryboat at Harwich. The ample-breasted blond woman behind the counter in the waiting room quickly sent a boy with the indispensable cup of morning tea, as I sat

down to wait for the bus. The manager of the airport, in his immaculate white gold-braided uniform, had spotted my name on the passenger list and, his waxed mustache bristling in his young black face, smiled and said, "We have been expecting you, sir." He whisked my luggage through customs and had it put in his private car. Proudly he gave me his card, on which his name was printed, followed by the initials M.B.E. (Member of the British Empire). Obviously I was *persona grata* here in this country, where hardly anybody ever sets foot unless he has something specific to do.

This narrow strip of land, bordering the Gambia River and nowhere more than 17 miles wide, is divided into the "Colony" around Bathurst and the "Protectorate" covering the rest of its 4,000 square miles, and extends like a 300-mile-long worm into the side of Africa. Since it is a separate territory, it has the whole machinery of government, complete with governor, chief secretary with his secretariat, financial secretary, attorney general, etc. The whole setup seems very much like that of a Gilbert and Sullivan operetta, including its vigorous movement for independence with a confused program which boils down to: "Give us independence, pay our debts, buy our supplies, and guarantee us a decent income."

The local press, which is a little difficult to read because it is so badly printed that all the characters run together, commented on a burning question of the moment as follows (and I quote literally):

Gambia Police Force. The recruitment of women to the Police Force is welcom only for the employement it will give to women and as contributing general to the relief of unemployment. We have no female troubles in the Gambia to warrant the employment of women constables otherwise.

And there are samples of utter confusion like:

Would it be necessary for us the share the Mali-system of government? This might do harm, though it would do good economically. . . . Is there any alternative to an association with Mali. Federation with Sierra Leone would be incongruous, even if it were practicable. To wait and see may not be an alternative. But what is of moment, is independence. We could then develop so as to be able to act in the future from a position of strength [The Gambia *Echo,* July 25, 1960].

While riding into the sleepy little city of Bathurst, however, I had the impression that most of the oratory about independence was mere rhetorical fireworks and that Bathurst might be first on a list of places where one could sit out the twentieth century—this invention of devils—without too much violence and die a peaceful death from old age or boredom under one's mosquito net. Streets are bordered by old colonial stone buildings with colonnades and galleries, and are laid out in comfortable squares along the wide Gambia River. Herds of cattle graze on the sparse grass between beach and houses. The Africans look like those in Dakar, but in slow motion. Here the African face still has a pastoral calm underlying a weary smile. They appear as though they dance in dream tempo a pastoral dance of life.

The early nineteenth-century buildings have lost their smell of slavery but it never was the slavery of the stinking holds of slave ships or of the dying in dungeons which still permeates Cape Coast in Ghana. Here the aura is something like the cozy slavery of old copper engravings, where the benevolent gentleman in knee breeches has just bought a naked savage, who looks up at him with adoring eyes. Bathurst actually breathes benevolence. I am not sure whether the Governor told me that it was fifteen years or fifty years ago that the last murder had been committed: "At any rate the last one we heard about," he said with a smile.

In the afternoon heat I drove to the end of town, where ancient sailing ships of age-old Portuguese design were being repaired in order to be loaded with the groundnut harvest from upriver. Groundnuts are the only crop which is grown for export and the precarious economy of the Gambia is entirely dependent on this peanut harvest.

On the way back to the hotel I had to fulfill my first duty as visitor to the Gambia. I drove into a small private park, where under huge ancient trees the government house stands. On a parapet below the mediocre Victorian mansion, six antique cannons dominate the wide placid river. A sentry, red-fezzed and with a red bolero over his khaki shirt, an old-fashioned rifle with bayonet in hand, stood streaming with perspiration in his little wooden sentry box. At the end of the lawn there was a small sign with an arrow saying simply, "The Book." In a tiny square booth of white brick, looking a little too much like a public lavatory, lay, secured by a chain, a leather-bound visitors' book with weathered gold lettering, in which every visitor to the Gambia, if he is of any standing at all, places his name and qualifications. The same evening awaiting me at my hotel I found a letter with the British coat of arms in embossed gold. It was an invitation to lunch at Government House.

The hotel is modern and clean and belongs, like all the new and many of the old buildings, to a Lebanese who came to the Gambia as a peddler. All along the West Coast these Lebanese seem determined to prove that in countries where everybody is poor and easygoing and where all government schemes to bring prosperity habitually fail, it is still possible to make a lot of money by frugality, hard work, family sense, and a lack of the special inhibitions imposed by Anglo-Saxon codes of business morality. Every village has its Lebanese or Syrian general store and every city its Levantine smuggling organization, be it for booze or diamonds. But Lebanese as it may be in ownership, the hotel is most British in its management and it radiates that particularly British aura of boredom mixed with stiff-lipped xenophobia which can make British hotels nearly as bearable as concentration camps. The unfriendly fat manager and his unseeing wife and daughter have their little clique gathered around them and the place is strictly stratified in bar and lobby and dining room. It is amazing how the British middle class in its innumerable substrata have not only reduced the voice and its modulations into an instrument of discrimination and segregation, but have even developed a device which one could call the British eye. Just as the voice is used in order to not-communicate, the eye is used in order to not-see, or to see, at best, selectively. This British eye can unseeingly pierce six layers of humans in order to recognize in the seventh one of its own tiny substratum. And so through this hot hotel opposite the quiet glaring river, they walked around in their mutual snubbing society, building high walls between their luncheon tables on the terrace or, at most, guiltily exchanging shamefaced grimaces. Gambians may no longer be excluded, but here politeness and even a prudent exchange of greetings can be combined with segregation. You can sit with a man, when unavoidable, and build up your little wall right across the table.

Next morning I walked out of the hotel through the steaming glare of the nearly deserted Sunday streets to the harbor where the cutters, built as they were two hundred years ago, lie in the muddy bay below a dike in a sweating, Dutch landscape, covering miles and miles of the vast Gambia River. Women in yards of cotton wrap come down the dike carrying loads of wood and sugar cane. Shoals of gleaming black children cavort in the muddy water. I returned along the waterfront and with the cruel sun bearing down on me passed two miles of crumbling arcaded warehouses with large deserted courtyards, where once slaves rolled barrels of English gin for their masters. Flaked yellow paint hung like fish scales from baked stone façades. The green of the wooden gates has been melted by decades of beating sun into a sample chart of warm and cool, acid and poisonous, shades of green. Where there is a shady spot, something human is lying on the stones as if dead. A blind ancient Moslem in red fez and indigo toga, imprisoned in his own shell of darkness, feels his way across the deserted glaring street. The sentinel in his tiny box is still standing there as in many yesterdays with his ancient rifle and his streaming expressionless face. In a villa nearby, hidden in hibiscus bushes, someone is playing a Chopin waltz so slowly that I first mistake it for the *Marche funèbre.*

On the beach near the hotel I sat in the sand among myriads of shells so different from those on Long Island, and yet this too was my earth, here in far-off Africa. In the warm sand I felt as though I had always lived here. The sun was now veiled in luminous vapor, birds which were neither gulls nor crows fought for scraps of fish, and one of the old peanut boats, dirty white and faded green, drifted past on the imperceptible current of the river Gambia.

That Sunday afternoon the *Apape,* the mail boat which calls every six weeks, was arriving. And in the midst of the steaming somnolence of Bathurst a wild commotion sprang up around the pier, an island of madness and excitement in the general torpor. People in their Sunday best—the men in stiff navy-blue suits and purple ties, the women in crimson, pink, and blue satin and velvet—pushed one another through the narrow opening of the gates to catch a glimpse of relatives arriving or to embrace tearfully for the last time cousins going away to "U.K.," as Britain is always called. Porters with unmanageable loads of luggage on their heads jostled their way through the crowd, and suitcases exploded on the cobblestones, spilling clothing, textbooks, and toiletries. Policemen with whistles gestured to distant trucks which were stuck in the crowd. Little girls, black dolls in old-fashioned organdy dresses, were hollering for their lost mammies, who in turn ran around frantically in search of their children.

The arrival of the *Apapa* is to Bathurst what the bullfights are to Madrid or the World Series to New York—an excuse for excitement and an emotional catharsis.

At the hotel they were all sitting within their little walls, waiting for the Sunday lunch of "Brown Windsor soup, assorted-cold-meats or pork-and-applesause, and ice cream with Pompadour wafer. The coffee will be served in the lounge, ⅛ extra."

In the lounge Dr. John Carrol was waiting for me. He was the man who had arranged my lectures and film shows for the doctors of the Gambia. From America I had communicated with him as "Chief of the Dental Department, Bathurst, the Gambia"; I now found out that he was not only his own staff as well but also the only dentist in the territory. He is a very tall, very cultured young man with an intelligent, good-looking wife, who is a Sierra Leonian. Even when I phoned him I pictured him as a young blond Englishman. But John Carrol was as African as the river Gambia itself. Both Dr. and Mrs. Carrol were typical "been-tos." This is a West-African term of mild derision and envy, given to those who have lived and studied in Britain and who have acquired in many respects English atti-

tudes, although they are at the same time vigorous nationalists and temperamentally unable, thank God, to assimilate the stuffiness of Putney or Kew Gardens. Perhaps their nationalism is overcompensation for their basic alienation from the non-"been-tos." For these people have changed in their system of social values, in their clothing (it is not unusual to meet an African lawyer in striped trousers, with bowler hat and rolled umbrella under the burning sun of Nigeria or Ghana), and in their entire way of thinking, and often this cultural cross-fertilization brings fantastically brilliant results.

At his house, where Dr. Carrol had arranged a small party for me, I met some of the younger doctors and intellectuals of Bathurst. Most of them were of course "been-tos" like John and Ruth Carrol and a few were Englishmen who had chosen to tear down the walls, including a young agricultural engineer, who was teaching rice cultivation to the Mandingo farmers deep in the Protectorate. He had lost his heart to them and lived among them with his young pregnant wife. He felt useful, for rice might be the answer to the yearly famines which ravage the country after the money from the only cash crop, peanuts, is exhausted.

"Last week I was in one of our villages," he said, "and I arrived just at the time of prayer. These people are orthodox Moslems. But the Chief of the village got up to welcome me. 'Please,' I said, 'don't let me interrupt you. I can wait.' But the Chief said, 'Oh, no, you come here so rarely and I am very happy to see you. I can pray later, for you stay just a little while but Allah is there all the time.'"

One of the doctors mentioned my work at the Schweitzer Hospital. "If you mention the word Schweitzer in West Africa" —Dr. Carrol smiled—"you might as well have dropped a bomb." I had not even realized that people knew the *"Grand Docteur."* All at once they started to speak about Schweitzer and his attitude of rejection toward the "blacks." "But he has worked for these people all his life," I objected. "Yes," they said, "but condescendingly. Has he not written that all men are brothers, but that we are like children, his younger brothers?" "That was thirty-five years ago," I said, "and you must concede that Africa has evolved fantastically in those thirty-five years! He has helped innumerable people during his years in Lambaréné; why don't you attack those who did nothing? Why don't you attack your own doctors in all the big cities who think of nothing so much as their own advancement?"

At that moment Ruth Carrol appeared and led me to a sumptuous *smörgåsbord* which was the last thing one expected in Bathurst. But this too was symbolical, as were the excellent French wines, of the overpowering will of these educated Africans even in an isolated spot like the Gambia to be cosmopolitan, to burst the confinement of geographical and political isolation. Between mouthfuls, another young doctor, John Mahoney, whose father was one of the first Gambians to be knighted, kept kidding me about the "condescending Christian lily-white endeavor in Lambaréné." He had a face aflame with intensity, intelligence, and wit.

Everyone agreed that the Gambia had to become independent. How it would be kept going, nobody seemed to know. But just as anyone with a tic, a stutter, or a bad job in America now can tell you that all his misfortunes are due to childhood trauma, in Africa all misfortunes are blamed on colonial governments, who never gave enough education, invested enough capital, or provided sufficient medical services. I said this. But, my friends pointed out, "It is too late now to theorize. Africa is awake, and for better or worse we want to take our destiny in our own hands. We know Paradise will not ensue. We know that the old earth of Africa is unkind, sick with erosion, and exhausted. We know there is comparative overpopulation already and that in forty years so many more mouths will have to be fed, it would be a miracle if the standard of living could be raised much above the present subsistence level. But we have chosen. . . ."

"Maybe you could start communes the way the Chinese do it," said the leftish English technician with the thin Saxon face. "No, we couldn't" said the surgeon. "Africa is not Asia. Our people are neither frugal nor are they hard-working. The Chinese system could only work if we imported Chinese! And that is precisely what they would want! But who knows, our cultural patterns have changed so much in the last sixty years, maybe we'll change radically in this respect too."

The head nurse of the Bathurst hospital was fat and jolly. Her wide dark face looked strong, stubborn, and humorous. "I want you to come and look at my house," she said, "I just built a new house." And we continued our party in the brand-new big house of poisonous green stucco which looks out over the harbor, where scores of sailboats lay in the luminous ebb tide as in a seventeenth-century Dutch drawing. Women were wading through the mud, their thighs dripping, gathering clams.

The Carrols and the Director of Medical Services, one of the first African doctors in the Gambia, had been invited with me to Government House. To me this was just an interesting adventure; to them it meant involvement in a conflict of conscience. On the one hand they enjoyed their standing as notables, on the other they felt that they were on enemy territory and might be regarded as traitors by other Gambians. Government House, or "Gee Aitch" as everybody calls it—how unbearably stuffy it must have been in the heyday of colonialism!

We were received on the steps of the pompous outside staircase by a most gracious figure in much too short Palm Beach trousers and a ridiculously old-fashioned Norfolk jacket. He had a long turkeylike neck and a small and lively, exquisitely carved thin head, adorned by a too small gold monocle. Carried along on a wave of courteous greetings pronounced in nearly inaudible Oxford tones, we met finally a second figure, much less alluring but more twentieth-century, whom I later identified as the Governor.

In the vast, nearly empty drawing room servants in red and white livery handed us drinks and cigarettes. In the conversation I dropped the name of a former Education Officer in the Gambia whom I had met elsewhere in Africa, John O'Halloran. It was he who had stimulated my desire to visit this little country. John O'Halloran had done a remarkable job in the Gambia, but was a rather original personality and far from a yes-man. I noticed a slight frown on the Governor's face. "Oh, yes, I remember O'Halloran, a rather eccentric fellow," he said with a polite sneer, and I felt it was more tactful to chat a bit about the history of British colonization along the river. Later in the vast, elegant, but dilapidated dining room the chicken was served, bathed in a paste of pallid starch from which some green peas emerged. But a very good Moselle wine could be used to wash it down painlessly. The service was silent and the conversation desultory. From the walls Queen Victoria and Edward VII watched us resignedly. From their faded gold frames a little sliver of gilt danced down an oblique sunray into my soup.

It developed that the gracious *ancien régime* figure with the monocle was the Governor's A.D.C. I had the impression he was far from a Colonel Blimp and that in his perfect Oxford accent he was trying to convey by a subtle code of understatement and carefully chosen platitudes his humanitarian concern and his essentially progressive ideas. One could imagine him taking off his slightly ridiculous Phileas Fogg outfit at night and reading works of sociology, anthropology, and the history of art in the silent evening hours of G.H. And indeed, in my remaining days at Bathurst I met him daily on the beach, hardly recognizable in sunglasses, an old khaki hat, and frayed shorts, with a towel over his arm and sandals in hand, walking a few miles to his favorite lonesome swimming spot.

I was strangely touched by this lunch at Government House. The dogged preservation of a style in the run-down mansion, this ghostly evocation of an empire which had already passed into history, was full of a melancholy charm and breathed the nobility of lost causes. Yet G.H., one felt, was well in touch with the changing patterns around it. I even wondered if its occupants took their own impoverished pomp seriously or if they danced their minuet out of obstinate loyalty while searching for practical solutions to today's problems.

The afternoon air was leaden with a brewing thunderstorm. A black sky pressed down on the indigo river and only the gleam of breakers, white and knifelike, two miles out, separated the heavens from the water. Nothing stirred, but the thunderstorm never came. At dinner on the hotel terrace they served roast beef and Yorkshire pudding while myriads of mosquitoes bored through one's socks and everyone discreetly rubbed his ankles under the tables. The nauseating café-concert music from the manager's three-record collection transformed the night into a comatose inferno of boredom.

When next morning I drove with Dr. Carrol into the Protectorate, I remarked that the road looked very much like the one we had taken from the airport. "No wonder," said Carrol, "there is only one road." The country lay flat, hot, and dusty, with patches of suburban trees, coarse grass, and low groundnut plants as far as one could see. The only majestic thing about the Gambia is the river from which it takes its name. Around the villages women were wading knee-deep in the mud, tending their rice. Men were not to be seen until you entered a village, where they were hanging around the market place or lying on the *bantabà*. The *bantabà* is a platform, erected in every village under the most widespread tree, where the men, draped in their long gowns, lie in the shade, conversing interminably or playing draughts. Meanwhile the women do the agricultural work, carry heavy loads of firewood to their houses, suckle their children, and have their bodies eaten by mosquitoes and leeches in the rice fields.

Rice is a fairly recent import and British agricultural experts, such as the engineer I met at the Carrols', are trying to teach the Gambians to plant it wherever possible in order to abolish the hungry season in which every year people still die from starvation. For every pound of groundnuts harvested is sold for export and the farmers have consistently refused to grow more, which could be used to supplement their own diet until the next harvest; they count on the government to feed them in the interval. Now the government is trying everything to make them self-sufficient the year round. The groundnut money, which averages some $60 a year per family, is used for clothing, feeding, and buying wives. But a nonviolent social revolution has taken place and now the women reserve whatever money they make from rice and palm kernels for themselves.

Not far from Bathurst, I saw some victims of the hungry season at the Medical Research Council Station, a converted military hospital, where young British doctors and biochemists were doing research in blood chemistry. To this small, meticulous hospital they generally admit those cases of mysterious edemas and heart failures—very frequent in young people in the Gam-

Gambia   Bathurst Beach

bia—which may well be related to the annual "hungry season."

The atmosphere in the hospital was serious and very gentle, that specifically British quality of seemingly hesitating, but quite purposeful gentleness one meets so often in the higher strata of British academic life.

Notwithstanding a gruesome history full of raids and sneak attacks on the early adventurers into the country, the present-day Gambians reflect a similar gentleness. They have an incomparable quiet charm, they are friendly and delightfully mannered. O'Halloran told me much about them. As Education Officer in the Gambia he had worked toward the ideal of teaching every Gambian child to read and write. In order to do so he had devised his own system of writing the Mandika language, the language spoken by some thirteen million Mandingos, who live in the Gambia and spill over into neighboring Senegal as well as South into Portuguese Guinea and Guinea, even extending into Sierra Leone. In 1947, when O'Halloran had first come to the Gambia, only 200 people attended school outside of Bathurst. O'Halloran not only created schools all over the Protectorate, but he also set up a teacher's training college at Yundum, where at one time the Government had tried to initiate a so-called "egg scheme," one of the many schemes for improving the Gambia's one-crop economy, which failed. The chickens died of epidemics and the Gambians blamed the government.

In the abandoned henhouses O'Halloran started to train the teachers who by now have fanned out all over the Gambia.

O'Halloran, himself, wrote nearly all of the entire existing literature in the Mandika language, which consists of a dictionary, an anthology of folk tales, and some simple textbooks on agriculture and hygiene. He went into the backwoods and organized schools; often when he returned the school had disappeared and the buildings, modest huts, had fallen into disrepair. "After all," the chiefs said, "we only started the school to please you, and when you are not here you don't enjoy it anyway." Girls were forbidden by their parents to attend O'Halloran's schools and the first girl, very keen on education, had to be kidnaped by her brothers in order to study there. After she was graduated the father forgave her, but declared that she was no longer his daughter since she had been entirely spoiled by education.

One of O'Halloran's best pupils—from a totally illiterate family—breezed through secondary school in three years, was sent to London to study English literature, and is now a headmaster in the Gambia. Looking at my audience of Gambian doctors and nurses I all at once realized that the younger ones among them might well have been products of O'Halloran's efforts, although his name was hardly remembered. In this way Africa, with its lack of historical sense, with its vegetation overgrowing all monuments within a few years, with its elements disintegrating every building except the huge slave castles of the West Coast, absorbs all influences, while forgetting from where they came or who the people were who gave their lives to this all-devouring continent.

The Gambia, a British colony and protectorate, is a narrow, twenty-mile strip which runs 300 miles inland along the banks of the River Gambia and is bounded on three sides by Senegal. Its capital is Bathurst, its population about 300,000, and the religion is for the most part Moslem. The Gambia River is the main means of transport, for there are only about 40 miles of hard-surface roads.

The Gambia was discovered by the Portuguese in 1455. In the early seventeenth century the British found their way inland, after which Portuguese, Dutch, and British interests wrangled for the country's trade for some 300 years. Bathurst was founded in 1816 and the colony was governed as part of Sierra Leone until 1888. The Protectorate (all of the country except Bathurst and Georgetown), created in 1902, covers 4,000 square miles.

The Gambia is ruled by the Executive Council, which consists of the Governor and a partly elected Legislative Council. The proportion of elected members has been constantly increased and Africanization of the Civil Service is progressing rapidly. In 1960 the Protectorate participated for the first time in elections for a house of representatives.

Since the soil is poor and sandy, agricultural possibilities are limited, and the economy of the Gambia has been dependent on one crop, peanuts. Recently British efforts have resulted in a secondary crop, rice.

The usual shortage of medical help prevails. In 1945 the government took over elementary education from the missions, and although school attendance is high in the Bathurst area only 50 per cent of the children in the rural areas go to school.

3 / Sierra Leone: Diamonds in the Garden

The Viscount turbo-prop flies the 400 miles between Bathurst and Freetown in an hour and a half, but only when you have landed does the real trip begin. After the compulsory farce with the visa people and customs has been performed—a farce eagerly taken over by even the smallest and newest countries—a waiting bus takes you to the "launch" to cross the bay to Freetown proper.

It is the rainy season. The sky is black over banana groves and cocoa bushes. The bus plods through puddle after puddle over the country road past primitive mud huts. Although it is not raining, every plant is dripping. At the pier the "launch" is waiting. It is a pitiable old motorboat designed for some fifteen passengers, but there are more than thirty with mountains of luggage. Complete confusion! Half the passengers fill the little cabin, the other half crowd in the open part of the tiny old boat, a few of them are struggling to get on top of the cabin. Then the arguments start as to where to put all the luggage: it is shoved behind benches, it fills up the leg space in the cabin, it is stacked on the tiny deck. The water of the bay is wild, and seemingly infinitely far away loom the Lion Mountains which gave Sierra Leone its name.

The overloaded launch is at last ready to leave. The engine stutters fearfully. A last suitcase is flung aboard. In the cabin, the middle-class English couples, back from leave, practice stiff-upperlip. Nobody speaks, and only an African baby is hollering. The mother flicks out a breast to quieten it. The boat has hardly started when from the ink-black sky the downpour begins. Sierra Leone rain is not rain at all; it is an opaque curtain of water, which crushes you and closes off everything from view. Ghosts of fishing boats skim past, their inverted triangular sails looming for a second through the water curtain. My plastic raincoat protects all of me, except my feet which are standing in an ever deepening puddle. When I open the doors of the cabin to fling my soaking camera case onto the luggage heap in the middle, I see the silent passengers inside as wet with sweat as I am with rain. In the shark-infested wild water the boat is tossed about, an overloaded nutshell.

"How much longer is this going to take?" I ask the crewman who is trying to fix a ridiculous shred of tarpaulin over our heads. "A bit more than half an hour, sah," he shouts in my ear, "to Government Wharf."

Suddenly the water curtain is torn away and the Lion Mountains, bright emerald in sun and mist, rise high above the boat. The door of the cabin is thrust open and fifteen pale, drawn faces stare out silently. The baby has abandoned the long black breast and is again hollering. The boat creeps up along the shore to Government Wharf. Freetown looks like a nineteenth-century engraving of an exotic port, a city building upon

itself as its old stone houses clamber up from the shore over the backs of older stone houses.

My host, John Akar, shouts an order and four black men in tatters gather our soaking luggage and haul it to his car. Without a word he throws them four pennies.

Freetown is now bathing in sunlight and steam. Enormous women in purple and yellow wraps waddle through the puddles majestically, balancing large loads of mangoes and cassavas on their heads, like eccentric royal tiaras. Naked children play in the muddy puddles in the middle of the streets. Decrepit open buses fly past them as if trying in vain to collide with each other. In spite of its dilapidated air and its repulsive dirt, the town is beautiful. There are solid Victorian stone buildings, sometimes gracefully Caribbean in style, with wrought-iron balconies as in New Orleans. Almost perversely all those elegant, African-Victorian dream castles are crowned with hideous red corrugated roofs. The paint, alternately baked by merciless sunshine and soused by vicious rains, hangs flaked and wrinkled from the shutters.

I expected to stay at the run-down City Hotel, but my host laughed at me. "That is the worst hotel in the world," I was told. We went to Government Rest House, which is built like an American motel and has a good dining room. Very unlike the Atlantic Hotel in Bathurst with its invisible walls between black and white and white and white, here the races and classes mingled spontaneously. There was not a trace of servility in the Africans or of superiority in the whites. Wherever independence is near or already accomplished, a subtle change takes place in those whites who have decided to stay on. It seems as though they too feel liberated from their compulsory superiority and do their best to be liked by the Africans and to be accepted on a purely human level.

25

A trip around Freetown ("the Colony") or into the interior ("the Protectorate") makes one wonder why this most beautiful spot in West Africa is not crowded with tourists. Mountain roads circle the Freetown peninsula and from every spot one has a view of the enormous bay, where during World War II three hundred warships found shelter at one time. On the high mountains above the city, Fourah Bay College, the oldest cultural institution in West Africa (founded in 1824), dominates the scene. In the teeming streets hundreds of Lebanese shops, which monopolize the retail trade, carry on their loud and hectic business. In innumerable hovels without light, water, or sanitation, human life is lived passionately and gaily. From these hovels come the leaders of the new Africa; a brilliant, cultivated young surgeon pointed with pride to his birthplace in old Freetown—a house of mud, corrugated iron, and bits of string!

Six or seven beaches surround Freetown, one more Tahitian than the other. If this is the famous white man's grave, it is the pleasantest grave imaginable.

At one of the little drinking clubs, founded in order to circumvent still-British licensing laws, I met an Indian-looking lad who, playing the international *bon vivant* to perfection, made it very clear that he knew his Paris, his New York, and his London. He had studied law in England and America and after the fourth Coke he insisted that we should visit his house. We stopped at an Edwardian mansion in the center of Freetown, all fluted columns and cement ornaments, painted a hideous yellow. Over

an ornamental outside staircase our host led us into a vast drawing room which was full of people. His father, a huge, monarchal man with a sallow complexion and an impressive hook nose, arose to greet us in a caricature of Oxford English. He wore khaki shorts over his mighty hairy thighs. My friend's stepmother, much younger, olive-skinned and deferent, addressed me in French. On the walls hung comically vulgar oleographs of Swiss lakes. Two greasy Levantine cousins entertained me in French platitudes. The patriarch in khaki shorts absent-mindedly frowned, smiled, and drummed his fingers on the arm of his chair. Lemonade was being served and then an African entered in a red fez and a pink nightshirt over expensive gray flannel trousers. He was all smiles, a round fat ball of smiles and cunning eyes.

"This is Paramount-Chief So and So," the lawyer son whispered into my ear. The chief and the patriarch began to talk to each other very rapidly, the chief smiling, the patriarch frowning and drumming. A German couple I had not noticed yet, shy and peasantish, took their leave. The cousins continued to smile with their fat faces.

"*Ça vous plaît,* Freetown?" the wife said mechanically in Lebanese French. "*C'est gentil, n'est-ce pas?*"

After I had left with a Sierra Leone doctor who had come along I asked him: "Who on earth are these people?"

"Oh," he said, "we were received by one of the most powerful men in the country. He is very rich and has very important legal businesses all over Sierra Leone, which in reality are just a cover for his illegal ones." "Like what for example?" I asked. "Oh, diamonds of course. The fat chief is one of his buddies. They smuggle diamonds together. One night police dug up a few hundred thousand dollars worth of diamonds in his garden, but he was able to prove that he did not put them there and that he had nothing to do with it and so everything is going on smoothly again."

Diamond smuggling has long been the most important racket of Sierra Leone and has cost the Sierra Leone government untold millions of revenue. It is now slowly being brought under control, or so they say.

We were walking through the rain. Huge red, yellow, and green segmented umbrellas, the size of garden umbrellas, bobbed up and down the shiny, hilly streets. We sought refuge in the Museum, which stands opposite the famous cotton tree in the center of Freetown. The cotton tree, which may well be over a thousand years old, looks like an enormous fort with projecting ramparts. It embodies the whole history of Sierra Leone: under its branches slaves were sold never to return, here African justice was meted out, and later its leaves rustled with the joyous sounds of freedom when the liberation of the slaves was celebrated.

The Museum is the former railroad station, a room of 30-by-30 feet with documents concerning Sierra Leone and its history and some moderately interesting sculpture, especially the so-called Nomolis, stone fetishes representing hideous seated male and female figures of unknown origin. The farmers of the Mende tribe find them in the earth and believe they are fashioned by the Supreme Being Himself. They are still highly feared and respected as harvest gods. Sometimes they are ceremoniously whipped to increase the harvest.

There was a medal commemorating the abolition of slavery. It says: "We are all brethren, 1807." I also found an ordinary Bols gin crock, displayed with the legend: "Old German Relic found in alluvial diamond rocks, of unknown date." In a showcase by itself stood an empty little pedestal labeled: "Model of the largest diamond found in Sierra Leone" and below it on a separate slip: "Stolen from the Museum on August 31, 1958."

Africa always has a touch of the comical. It often shocked me in its cruelty and harshness, but even then it was not tragic: there was always some dissonance in the cruelty or the harshness, which made it tragicomic. The continent itself seems to be bathed in raucous laughter, but, make no mistake, African laughter is not always a sign of amusement. It may become without warning a prelude to violence. For laughter in Africa may also be reaction to bafflement, a defensive tensing of the facial muscles, or an apology. African laughter, African dancing, African clothing, and African sculpture—even African politics—have something in common: the grotesque.

Children of three or four years already make the grotesque dancing steps which Negroes have imported into America and America in turn has exported to the rest of the world: the hiccuping obscene thrust of the buttocks, legs and arms in orgiastic rhythm. Even the African offbeat taste in clothes has here and there survived in America among sections of the Negro population: the striped purple and white jacket, very tightly fitted, the gold lamé trousers, the purple top hat. There is no clothing extravaganza which cannot be seen in Africa. But no one in Africa ever feels badly dressed and the most incongruous rags are worn together, one on top of another. After all, there is no tradition of being clothed at all. Rags and tatters do not seem to look disreputable to anyone. The only exceptions to this are the newly Westernized intellectuals and politicians who, having studied abroad, invariably dress in the most conservative English style, complete with quiet tie and waistcoat, even under the hottest sun. But it is ever so much more normal to wear a poisonous blue plastic coat, with hood, and on top of that a sun helmet. Or an elegantly torn, black silk evening blouse and a yellow cotton skirt full of slogans of Independence with large portraits of popular political leaders dancing on the buttocks.

A baby is fastened on the back in a lavender and orange shawl, and the lady's feet are shod in acid-green plastic sandals from Bata, with torn straps.

Street names too have a—consciously or unconsciously—humorous turn: Johnny Bright Lane is the dirtiest possible narrow mud track between two rows of hovels.

Next to the undertaker ("We bury you dead") is a "Psychic Health Institute," a dirty building which seems to be the headquarters of a vulture union. I counted one day forty vultures sitting on it, their long bare necks hopefully extending and contracting. Vultures are everywhere in Freetown. I used to abhor them with conventional revulsion. I do no longer. Vultures do not harm anything alive and they clean up what must be cleaned up: all that is dead. It is our perverted sense of values that makes us admire the violent destructiveness of more "heroic" animals —applaud the eagle who kills the mouse and the lion who strikes down an antelope—and detest the vulture who lives on what suffers no more. In Freetown I developed a liking for these gentle, carnivorous birds. The Africans seem to agree with me. Everywhere the vulture's services are highly appreciated and killing a vulture is punished severely.

Night in Freetown is an "Arabian Night": the hundreds of little stalls of the kola-nut vendors and soft-drink parlors are aglow with small smoking oil lamps. Long-robed figures move in throngs to the rhythm of muted laughter which sometimes swells into shouting or swearing. Next to "Gab's Free and Easy. Coffins in all Sizes," "What profiteth it a man . . . ?" a record shop is giving free concerts. Teen-agers dance their erotic dances in the street. Moslems kneel on the muddy sidewalks and bow eastward, touching the ground with their foreheads. A group of celebrants of a burial come dancing out of a dark side street, beating drums and brandishing acetylene lamps. At the bar of the City Hotel young black lawyers are getting drunk and practicing their Oxfordest English on one another and on the few remaining bleary-eyed Englishmen.

In Government Rest House there is a sign informing guests that "A first class gentlemen's hairdresser is in attendance on Thursdays. Haircuts 3 sh. per capita." Since I was going to meet the Prime Minister on Thursday afternoon I decided to have my *caput* tidied, but it really was not necessary. In the garden of the old villa, which is Sir Milton Margai's residence, his driver was cleaning the big old Humber. A policeman showed me into a large bare room. On a dresser stood a rare Sierra Leone sculpture, a box of chocolates, and a large nude, pink celluloid doll which could open and close its eyes. Threadbare comfortable chairs stood around as though for a conference or a family gathering. No one showed up. Then an old man with the face of an African Gandhi, in baggy trousers and smoking a big pipe, came shuffling down the hall. "An old relative," I thought, but it was of course Sir Milton. His face, folds of old black skin over projecting bones, with very lively eyes, lit up in a kind, intelligent smile. As he slumped down in one of the big old chairs, he grinned: "Whisky or a soft drink?" A boy in shirt sleeves and with bare feet brought orangeade and that was the end of protocol.

Sir Milton, who was born in 1895 in a small village in the Protectorate, was educated in England and has been a doctor in almost every district of Sierra Leone. He was the first doctor from Sierra Leone to get a European degree, and his brother was the first Sierra Leonian to receive a British law degree. He had seen all the living and dying for forty years all over his country until he retired into politics in 1950. Pomp and circumstance, cavalcades and Rolls Royces do not impress him. He is profoundly human and eminently practical and quietly has steered his course to the top, in complete contrast to the glaring show-

MICHEL ABOUDER

Franek Freetown 3 VII 60

manship of Nkrumah or the cold efficiency of Sékou Touré.

Sierra Leone has the oldest tradition of learning on the West Coast, and the Creoles of Freetown—which here means the descendants of freed slaves, mostly of mixed ancestry but with British citizenship—are as proud and cultivated a group of people as one can meet anywhere. Although the 27,000 Creoles are now politically subordinate to the people of the Protectorate who outnumber them ten to one, it is the Creoles who have given the pronounced British style to public life.

Sir Milton did not talk politics. He was not the Prime Minister at the moment, but the old doctor interested in improving the health of Sierra Leone, and he had all the facts in his head. Thirty years ago this man had penetrated the female secret societies in the wild upcountry, the so-called Bundu societies, to which all girls belong and into which they are initiated at puberty by the cruel rite of female circumcision, a practice still existing all over black Africa. Step by step Dr. Margai was able to introduce the principles of modern midwifery into the puberty initiation teachings of the society.

For boys, also, the initiation ceremonies culminate in circumcision, which, after a long period of preparation, the boy has to undergo without flinching. When the boys reach puberty, the "Porro Devil" comes and lures them into the bush. There they have to go through the ordeals which will make them into men. The initiation formerly took many months, but now it has been reduced to a few weeks. It is a training course in self-control and

a grounding in the responsibilities of adult life. Moral codes are taught by practical examples and traditional songs and dances of the tribe are inculcated.

It is easy to scoff at these ceremonies as "primitive," but there is more to initiation than a cruel rite. I question whether the total absence of rites of passage from one stage of life to another is not a weakness of our culture. Perhaps this absence contributes to the general confusion of values often resulting in juvenile delinquency.

Male circumcision has also its hygienic rationale, but how to explain the cruel custom of clitoris excision in the girls? It has been said that the reduction of sexual pleasure would make the girls more faithful. But if this is the objective, the Bundu societies might as well give up the operation! Although virginity before marriage is thought to be very important in Sierra Leone,

adultery after marriage is so common that the husband's indignation has been codified into a price list. If caught in adultery one may have to pay the equivalent of the price of a chicken to the irate husband if it happened in the fields or of a sheep if caught in the house, but only when the lovers are surprised in the marital bed must the husband feel personally insulted and injured.

Another hypothesis—a psychological one—came from an African doctor with whom I discussed the custom. He felt that in a country where children are a valuable source of cheap labor and child mortality is high, it is an empirical way of forcing the sexual drives into a direction which is bound to produce children. Maybe the unconscious reasoning is: since exploratory sexuality and stimulation begin very early in African life, at puberty it is as if custom ordains, "Now go and make children."

France

John Akar, the young director of the Sierra Leone Broadcasting System, drove me to Songo, a small town in the Protectorate. John is a man from the Protectorate, from an isolated rural region, but in Sierra Leone this does not exclude a certain cosmopolitanism. His father is a Catholic, his mother a Moslem. "There can't be religious intolerance here, because in every family there are Christians of all the various brands, as well as Moslems and pagans," he says. John is African of course, but he is aware too of his Lebanese-Jewish-English heritage. He speaks B.B.C. English, and was also trained in America, where he appeared for a time as an actor on Broadway. He does some play-writing and is busy with innumerable other cultural activities. All this together represents the portrait of an African nationalist, who believes his country could be an Eden, if it would grow into a "planned democracy." This euphemism is used all over Africa to describe anything ranging from total tyranny through a one-party government to a pseudo-parliamentary system with jailed opposition. The niceties of parliamentary elections and loyal oppositions are a fiction on a continent where more than 80 per cent of the voters are illiterate. Political programs mean very little to them and their loyalties are to their tribe and their clan.

John Akar believes that with mechanized farming his country could become rich, and, below the rising road, he pointed out the huge fallow fields which could bear cocoa crops and the endless mangrove swamps which his imagination saw converted into rice fields. John thinks, of course, that one day he will be a minister and probably a prime minister. This is not at all unlikely. So firmly rooted in so many ethnic groups and religions, so pliable and sophisticated and such a good speaker, he is one of the handful of available young men who have an even and unprecedented chance to scramble to the top.

Africa is now the land of unlimited possibilities. To rise from sergeant to general may take a week, from college student to minister may take a month, and from country doctor to prime minister a few years. It is all quite normal on this continent in mutation. For mutation rather than revolution is the word which describes what is happening in Africa. In every corner of Africa, institutions and aspirations make uncontrolled leaps from stone age to medieval level to mid-twentieth century. Where no wheel existed a few years ago, crazy buses now round corners at 80 miles an hour. From villages isolated since the dawn of history, people take planes to be treated at a hospital or to be educated at a university.

Of course the mutations are not limited to Africa. Elsewhere there has been the jump within sixty years from kerosene lamp to moon rocket. The rise of the non-whites within a few years from slavery and total subjugation to a dominant position on the world scene must be looked at as one of the great biological upheavals.

One of the new mammals was shown to me, when I had my audience with the Minister of Health. A burly man in a sumptuous, Victorian-style office, he seemed secretive and sly. He was slumped behind a big mahogany desk, his fez slightly awry on his bullet head, his pinkish nightshirt-like *agbada* sweeping the floor. His Excellency's hand was playing with a shepherd puppy at his feet and he avoided giving me any replies. His Scottish aide sometimes took over and answered some of the medical questions I hoped to get explained. When I mentioned this enigmatic attitude to other doctors they defended him hotly: "The man is not secretive at all, he is a very nice fellow. He just has absolutely no idea what to say. Two years ago he was still the traffic cop in front of the very building he is throning in now. But he is a chief and he does have political power and has been given a job. So what can you do? . . . We have our good people, we have our Margais, but for the time being we'll have to manage with this fellow." "Don't worry," I replied, "our Ike once started his cabinet with twelve millionaires and a plumber!"

The road to Songo went through John Akar's projected Eden, rising from swamps and jungles into villages of round mud huts. The old huts were still thatched, the newer ones topped with the corrugated iron roofs which make contemporary African villages so ugly, but prevent the massive fires in which old villages go up in flames at the drop of a match. It had rained all night, and beyond the mud-spattered vegetation along the road banana trees and cocoa shrubs were green and lush. We stopped at a brook where women were doing their laundry, cleaning themselves in the bargain. The rainy season is the season of cleanliness; in the dry season the water is so rare you have to buy it by the bucketful. Giggling women came to look over my shoulder at my drawing and shouted with delight when they recognized themselves. A girl of twelve, disappointed that I had not done justice to her budding breasts, pulled at her young nipples to show me and was radiant when I had improved her contours.

The road was lined both with flowers in clusters, tall as young birches, and with car wrecks every mile or so. Africans can buy cars now (don't ask me how, on an average yearly earning of $150), but who will repair them? Sierra Leone seems to have the highest car insurance rate in the world, which is not surprising, because after one weekend I found six fresh wrecks adorning the approaches to Freetown. They are probably still lying there as a silent tribute to progress: why tow them away and with what? At a particularly treacherous turn there was a sign, "Danger!" with a huge skull for emphasis. The wide road dipped and narrowed over a one-lane bridge: a mousetrap set on a waterfall.

Below on the rocks, among some rusty relics, a truck and a new car were lying with their legs in the air like dead beetles.

Songo, a village of mud houses neatly laid out in squares, is some miles from the highway, and can be reached only by a dirt road between fields of cocoa, yam, rice, and beans. Evening was beginning to fall and on the porch in front of every house men were relaxing in hammocks, while the women, neatly dressed in starched royal blue and magenta dresses with flounces, were preparing supper on small wood fires. John walked around with his transistor radio going full blast, calling greetings to everyone. He was electioneering for the distant future. The black eyes on the porches followed us smilingly or seriously, but never aggressively, in the mild evening light. The atmosphere was as clean as the meticulously swept streets. Serenity and satisfaction with life seemed to exude from the little village. "Here you don't need planned democracy, John," I said, "Eden is here already!"

We bought some kola nuts, which are used all over Africa to drive away exhaustion and hunger. But as an amateur African I only find them disgustingly bitter. At the station of the ridiculously narrow-track railway (2 foot 6 gauge), the panting toy train was being loaded with vegetables for Freetown. This is Sierra Leone's only railroad and, like San Francisco's cable cars, a source of amusement for everyone. A song about it is Sierra Leone's unofficial national anthem:

The train for Bo
She no agree for go
The engine she done tire
For lack of plenty fire
The train for Bo
She no agree for go.

French Freetown 3.VIII.60

Women of fairy-tale beauty were glowing in the dusk and the local whore shouted something provocative in pidgin English. The little middle-aged Lebanese shopkeeper stood in his doorway, proud of his full-breasted African wife in her harsh purple and green finery. She was not more than eighteen and had a light-skinned baby in her arm. The Lebanese traders often marry chief's daughters. This means an investment, for, although dowry must be paid to the Chief, he is an important relative to have. Also to the Chief this transaction is quite advantageous, because to him with his many wives it means unlimited credit at the only emporium in town.

It was nearly dark now. A motorcycle came rattling down the quiet wide street and stopped right in front of us, blocking our passage. For a moment I felt panicky, but all the man wanted was to shout to John Akar—whom he had recognized as the man from Freetown radio—that he should cut out the Beethoven stuff on the radio and instead play the record the cyclist had been requesting for months. . . .

Next morning, Dr. Vincent, an African dentist with a string of British degrees, walked with me through Freetown to show me the markets. The finest is King Jimmy's market, deep down on the beach where the vegetable boats were coming in from across the bay. I drew the scene from a viaduct in the higher city, from which the vegetable stalls and the brightly clad women looked like exquisitely arranged nosegays on the steps leading up from the beach. Buses flew past on the narrow viaduct, nearly hitting me and creating a draft that blew through the sheets of my sketching pad. At Krootown market the crowds were denser. We talked to the medicine vendor with his elaborate display of roots and pods and leaves and branches. His recipes were very specific: for gonorrhea, take this root, boil it four hours, sieve, and drink while warm; for stomach ulcer, powder these seeds, add cat's urine, and rub on your stomach; to prevent snake bites, rub your feet and legs with these leaves; for virility, take this powdered rhinoceros horn one hour before retiring. . . . This is partly nonsense, partly effective materia medica empirically arrived at after centuries of experimentation. Didn't our quinine come from native medicine, our tranquilizers from rauwolfia, our cocaine from medicinal leaves? The doctor showed me his native house on Savage Square, a hovel without water, light, or sanitation, where his parents, his brothers, his sisters, his aunts and uncles took up every inch of space and there was never any privacy. I looked at the man at my side in his London-made suit, his sensitive, wide African face smiling, a man who was so sensible and intelligent that I felt closer to him than to many people from my own home town. This can happen in one generation! In one generation human beings with their miraculous plasticity can pull themselves up from squalor and indignity to culture and sophistication. But also in one generation they can fall from the pinnacle of culture to the ritual mass murders of Auschwitz and Bergen-Belsen.

We walked past the church from which a funeral procession emerged. People were stiffly dressed in their Sunday best, the men in dark suits, the women looking like black replicas of small-town churchgoers in the Middle West. I shook hands with a curio dealer, whose pidgin English I didn't understand, but whose son appeared to be at Cambridge. I asked Dr. Vincent, "How do they finance his studies?" "The way we all do," he answered matter-of-factly. "Where there is no money and the boy has talent the whole family joins in, the whole clan. They invest in the boy and follow his progress eagerly. Then, once he has graduated, he is their proud possession. . . . Their investment has borne interest," he added ironically. "For the rest of his life he'll have to pay them back with money, with favors,

French VIII 60
Hauling in the nets

and by helping to finance the study and the businesses of his brothers, cousins, and second cousins. But that is all right, it is part of our growth."

I shook hands with Dr. Vincent, for I was late for an appointment with Dr. John Karefa-Smart, the Foreign Minister. This thin, tall man in his seersucker suit might serve as an antidote against all vapid generalization about Africa, new, old, or in-between. John Karefa-Smart studied medicine at McGill University in Canada, where he was graduated; he served in the Royal Canadian Medical Corps, received a Harvard degree in Public Health, and rose to regional director of the World Health Organization in Africa. He is also an ordained minister and probably one of the few ordained ministers who flies his own plane. This man of extraordinary poise and most urbane courtesy was born upcountry in the rural Protectorate, as was Sir Milton Margai. He radiates quiet strength and confidence.

A few days later I heard him deliver a keynote address at the World Youth Congress in Accra, Ghana. The university auditorium was filled to capacity with young people from all over the world, many from newly independent countries. The new African countries especially were represented by fiery youths in their national garb. Karefa-Smart's address was balanced and wise. He emphasized that any democracy worthy of the name had to be built on the sanctity of the individual and his rights and that no expedience justified violation of the dignity and freedom of one's adversaries. He was violently attacked by vicious heckling from the ultra-nationalistic youths, especially the Ghanaians, but he withstood all onslaughts without giving ground. How easy it would have been for him to inflame his audience by playing on their nationalistic fanaticism. Right there, in Ghana, he even alluded to the sacrilegious quotation from Nkrumah on his statue in front of Parliament House: "Seek ye first the political kingdom . . ." "We should," Karefa-Smart said to his audience with a smile, "not forget the other Kingdom in our search for the good for Africa."

Lumley Beach seems endless, with its palms blown obliquely inland by the eternal winds and its blue mountains in the distance shrouded in rain. The fishermen, squatting before their flimsy palm-leaf huts, are preparing their huge nets, more than a mile long. These wild-looking pagans are immigrants from Ghana, but they fish all along the West Coast. When the net was ready, they carried it out into the surf by rowboat from two points half a mile apart. Then they began to haul the net ashore with a row of fishermen at each end, forming a column with the shorter men and the naked children nearest the water, the tall men, some of them veritable giants, forming the rear. The net was hauled in slowly to the rhythm of a litany, eternally repeated, a hymn to the god of the sea. Not so long ago they still sacrificed virgins to their god. Endlessly the columns moved on, dancing forward and backward and at last the net was dragged on land, full of gold and silver creatures whose still shiny wide-open eyes reflected the sky. Then the women scrambled from the sand, gathered the fish in their baskets, and, balancing their loads on their heads, went off to the markets. Along the beach a million land crabs seemed to sense my steps, or did they see me with their large eyes on stilts on top of their square bodies? As I approached, they fled in formation hundreds of yards ahead, the huge comic legs moving sideways into the surf. I undressed to go swimming. The fishermen's bodies looked hard and black like polished ebony, and I felt vaguely ashamed of my pale and hairy skin. The wild surf and the undertow didn't seem to make much distinction between us. The rain was suddenly beating down on my clothes.

40

I was scheduled to leave Sierra Leone next day, but the charm of the country makes schedules illusory. I simply had to see the "Football Match of the Century."

It was the first football match I had watched since high school, and it was an extraordinary afternoon. To raise money for a new stadium the high civil servants and the ministers of Sierra Leone had formed themselves into two teams. Bravely, in the streaming rain the bald, fat dignitaries ran frantically after the ball, slithering through the mud, risking heart attacks and broken bones. The Prime Minister was to be the referee, but old Sir Milton had a cold and had to excuse himself at the last minute. All Freetown had to see the match; the road to the playground was blocked for hours and the Army was called in to direct traffic.

Before it started, two teen-age boys approached me hand in hand, "Excuse me, sah," said one with an orange cap, "we are most interested in the game, but unfortunately we find ourselves financially embarrassed. Could you perhaps give us a scholarship?" "Go climb a tree!" I said, less formally. Indeed, in all the trees around men and boys hung in clusters and risked their lives to watch. I saw one man fall from a branch, shrieking with laughter, when the Finance Minister, Mr. Mustapha, missed the ball and with one fat thigh extended in the air slid five yards on his behind through the mud. The Irish bishop sitting next to me, ex officio, held his belly and became dangerously purple. The Excellencies played as seriously as if their political lives depended on the game, and the whole population roared and rocked and shrieked in the healthiest kind of mass catharsis ever invented.

No book about Africa can completely dispense with a reference to cannibalism. It is still practiced no doubt, but it is taboo as a subject of conversation. Once in a while there is a scandal. There are remnants of "leopard" societies where old men, eager to restore their virility, hire a murderer, disguised as a leopard, to kill a youngster or a virgin. . . . A few years ago some forty-eight skulls were dug up in Ghana, and a respected doctor was implicated in the ritual mass murder. . . . A child was found in a pond in Accra with liver, eyes, and genitals removed. It turned out that the instigators of this ritual murder were devout so-called Baptist parents who wanted a potent charm to help their son pass his doctorate in London University! . . . But these are lapses into a "religious" cannibalism, not a culinary one. One might as well forget about missionaries made into croquettes for chiefs. Cannibalism is a method of magical self-protection. The "medicines" confer power over one's enemies or rivals, and are believed to guarantee success in dangerous undertakings. The *borfima* of Sierra Leone, a mixture of human intestinal fat and various organs, may still sometimes be made. "Young men are sometimes 'lost' at sea during fishing trips," said a Sierra Leone barrister with whom I could discuss this. Some time ago, a youngster who felt what was coming had prudently disappeared after he overheard that he had been prophylactically reported "lost" at sea.

"But why are you people so disproportionately horrified about our sporadic ritual murders?" the barrister asked me. "I don't defend them of course, they are throwbacks to an earlier cultural stage. Our leopard societies are dying out and we certainly help them to do so. But every time I meet a European or an American he gets as fast as he can to this tantalizing subject of ritual murder. We have not the monopoly, you know." He drank his Scotch slowly. "I'd like to remind you," he said, "that the ritual murder, this need for anointment with borfima oil, is an expression of helplessness and anxiety. Didn't your

Nazis dress up in barbaric uniforms and methodically go on a ritual murder spree, which lasted for years, on a scale no African witch doctor ever dreamt of? And they were not black primitives, illiterate peasants in backward villages, who make their magic ointments from a few unfortunates. The Nazis were lily-white gentlemen, scientifically manufacturing soap from millions of victims. And, didn't you Americans," the dispassionate Oxford voice continued, "drop a little bomb some time ago 'in order to save the lives' of your clan brothers? Didn't you sacrifice a pathetic couple because they had sold tribal secrets to the rival clan, who as it happened had known the atomic secret long before? Also, it is not so long ago that Europeans would steal parts of the clothing or the hair of an executed man as a charm. . . . Leave it to us to uproot the remains of our ritual murder and we'll leave it to you to uproot yours."

Sierra Leone, which covers 28,000 square miles, is about the size of Ireland. Its population is 2,100,000, of which 70,000 live in its capital, Freetown. There are three main regions: a coastal belt of mangrove swamps, stretches of wooded hill country, and an upland plateau. Freetown, the oldest city in West Africa, was founded in 1792 by freed slaves, returned from the New World and Britain. This city also houses West Africa's oldest institution of higher learning: Fourah Bay College, founded in 1824.

Independence was well prepared for by the British and was reached in April, 1961.

Power and prestige was traditionally in the hands of the Creoles concentrated in the old Crown Colony around Freetown. They are direct descendants of the freed slaves who settled Freetown in the early nineteenth century. In the present government, however, people from the inland Protectorate occupy the highest positions.

The religions are Moslem, Christian, and animist.

The major export is palm kernels; but ginger, cocoa, piassava, coffee, rice, chrome ore, and iron ore are also exported; as are diamonds, which are now being mined by machinery.

4 / Ghana:

Prima Donna of Freedom

The first time I arrived in Accra, it was in the middle of the night. The country had just become independent, and in the airport waiting room British civil servants were having a drunken good-by party before taking off for London. Grave and dignified Ghanaian policemen in their red fezzes were eying the Britishers without hostility, but with quiet contempt.

When my plane landed there again in 1960, eight Russian Ilyushins were lined up in front of an improvised grandstand. A military band was playing to honor Ghana's first casualty in the Congo, a policeman killed in a traffic accident.

Ghana is more than just a country. It is a symbol and a catalyst. When it became independent in 1957 it caused an earthquake which made tremble the seismographs in all colonial territories of Africa. It meant the beginning of the end of British, French, and Belgian Africa. And this was understood everywhere except in South Africa. Three years later official Ghana had not only become aware of its pioneering role: it had turned into the prima donna of "Free-dom!" The case of Ghana is special. It had long been one of the wealthiest African territories when it was still called the Gold Coast, and for good reason—the Ashanti Gold Fields Corporation processes some of the richest ore in the world. It had already developed a degree of political consciousness eighty years ago, at the time of Gordon's assassination at Khartoum. Kenya was then still an

42

impenetrable wilderness and Albert Schweitzer had just entered elementary school. In addition, whoever says "Ghana" says "cocoa," and every second bite of chocolate candy wherever eaten in this world means a small contribution to Ghana's economy.

Accra, the capital, is still a shantytown built of corrugated iron and mud, set in a sun-scorched ocher landscape, and teeming with 150,000 gay people in all shades of black, yellow, and white. Rising among and above the shanties are the skyscrapers. The enormous Ambassador Hotel, built in the style which by now should be called "airport-modern," could just as well stand in the heart of Cincinnati. On its terrace a most cosmopolitan flock of birds of passage is constantly chirping business deals. Next to beer-drinking German businessmen, who don't look too de-Nazified, Israeli engineers are discussing road-building contracts with Ghanaians draped in their native togas; a residual English official with a monocle chats with two Arabs in burnooses. An Indian doctor is conversing with the two Russian "technical advisers" with whom I share the dining table in the Government Hospitality Center. They are entertaining fellows, able to converse in perfect French and German. (When I asked them where they learned these languages so well, they answered with disarming sincerity, "We had five years of conversation courses at Political School, of course.")

I just missed talking with Dr. Kwame Nkrumah, to whom I had three letters of introduction from mutual friends. When I arrived at his palace I had hardly time to greet him before he jumped in his brand-new Rolls Royce to race to his equally new state yacht which was to take him to Liberia. He was going there to participate in one of the numerous conferences, where freshly baked chiefs of newly born African states are issuing unanimous communiqués while trying to outmaneuver one another in their ambitions to become the leader of a future Pan-Africa.

I had instead a conversation with Nkrumah's ultra-English private secretary, a well-shaped lady of about forty whom everybody had expected to become Mrs. Nkrumah until he imported and married an Egyptian girl. Between the Castle and the city of Accra itself stands a coldly modernistic Arch of Triumph, close to the notorious crossroad where on February 28, 1948, an English officer made the mistake of opening fire on demonstrators. This gave Nkrumah the opportunity to cable immediately London, demanding independence. Copies of this cable were astutely sent at the same time to the entire world press. The Arch of Triumph bears in proud lettering, "Liberty and Justice." Members of the now harassed Opposition Party point this out with a bitter grin. Close to the Arch, in front of the very modern House of Parliament, a clumsy statue of Kwame Nkrumah raises its right arm. In the pedestal the amazing inscription is chiseled: "Seek Ye First The Political Kingdom And The Rest Shall Be Added."

I attended a session of Parliament. It looked like a miniature imitation of a session of Parliament in London, executed in black, and with surprising variations on the parliamentary theme. The Speaker, a wide-faced, very dark Ghanaian, with the golden Mace lying solemnly before him, was flanked by his two clerks, all three wearing their white wigs, which contrasted wonderfully with the shiny dark mahogany of their skins. To the right of the Speaker, on the Government benches, some forty members were sitting, most of them dressed in rich gold-threaded national costumes. To his left, on the Opposition benches, only six members were present. I was told that thirty-eight members on that side had been "unavoidably delayed" because they were at the moment in prison.

The procedure matched the costume-party atmosphere. In general perfect British speech prevailed and there was an abundance of traditional exclamations and ejaculations: "Mr. Speakah, Mr. Speakah!" "Heah, heah!" or "Shame, shame!" But as soon as an Opposition Party member tried to open his mouth there was raucous African laughter and cries of "Sit down, you fool!" And, even stranger, after the Opposition member had tried in vain to shout indignantly against the storm, with the Speaker hammering his gavel constantly in order to stop him, the defeated man sat down roaring with laughter himself, tears of gaiety rolling down his cheeks. The matter under discussion, however, was not gay at all: a law was being voted which made it a crime, punishable by fifteen years' imprisonment, to publish "false information" against the Government.

As in England, it was strictly forbidden to take photographs or to sketch in Parliament. So I have to apologize for this little sketch scribbled under the table on the back of the "Order of the Day."

I make Ghana sound rather unattractive, but I have heard convincing arguments for the defense. Ghana inherited from the British a parliamentary system which even in Europe—despite a centuries-old development of tradition—still often proves ineffective. Ghana certainly was not ripe for it and Nkrumah had the impossible task of trying to create unity in a country which, traditionally divided into tribes under the rule of mighty chiefs, had not ripened to the idea of national co-operation and integration. One must expect that all over Africa for some time to come a national government will be represented by one strong man. The mass of the population is after all still illiterate and cannot be expected to be politically mature to the point where our own precarious democratic procedures can be successfully adopted.

There is general fear that the winds from the Sahara will bring direct fall-out to Ghana, but to judge from the reactions I heard in Ghana and Nigeria, it is certain that the political fall-out from French atom bomb tests in the Sahara may be more fatal to the position of France—and indeed the whole Western world—in Africa than any health hazards to the African peoples.

I took a taxi from Parliament House, but downtown we were stopped by a huge parade, demonstrating under the leadership of a cabinet minister, against the proposed French atom bomb tests in the Sahara. Large banners carrying the words, "Stop this Hell Bomb" and "Stop this murder move," were bobbing above the crowds. At last my taxi could proceed to the harbor of Accra, far away from the center of the city. Freighters cannot come close to the shore because of the tremendous surf. The ships were lying far off the coast and hundreds of heavy surf-boats rode the boiling breakers to and fro, each boat manned by a dozen or so half-naked muscular black paddlers who loaded and unloaded with a technique it must have taken generations to perfect. It looked like the old Africa of the slave trade still surviving. Sometimes a boat capsized, thrown off the foamy crest of a breaker. Then lifeboats would go out, not to save the men—who are excellent swimmers and anyway expendable—but to bring boat and cargo to safety. Heavy crates and huge casks are carried on heads and naked backs to the shore. Once the boats are empty, they return to the ships. Overseers, like slave-drivers of old, paced stony-faced through crowds of illiterate coolies, making notes. The working life of these boatsmen starts in childhood and they are usually finished at age thirty. Some of them become customs officials. One of these, a venerable graybeard who later in life had learned to read and write, became my friend and I drew him.

The population of Accra constantly delights the eye by the immense vitality and *joie de vivre* glowing in every face. Since Independence, the native toga has again become popular for men; the women never abandoned their native dress. These togas mean emphatically: "We are free and proud of our traditions." For gala occasions the "kente cloth," woven of gold thread and vividly colored silk, is worn. It may be much more expensive than a good Western suit, but it is worth it: against the dark skin it is immensely decorative, authentic, and dignified.

The women, loosely draped in colorful wraps which emphasize their impressive curves and bumps, are imposing. Slim and charming when young, they develop later into massive matrons and are called "mammies." The mammies of Accra, surrounded by their broods, monopolize "free enterprise" on a small scale.

And sometimes on not such a small scale. Large capitals are occasionally built up by the mammies in their ramshackle market shops. From sunrise until late at night they are behind their stalls, chattering, selling, gossiping, shouting, quarreling, and laughing with wild gestures which make their huge bellies, buttocks, and breasts shake like earthquakes. Two mammies fought like tigers to sell me three packs of Players! Tiny girls try to sell the little string of beads they made or sit all day on a curb with two grapefruit and a cucumber waiting for a customer. The mammies sometimes become quite wealthy and always fatter. The "mammy-cloth," billowing around their immense bodies, makes them look like walking advertising columns. There are, printed in a cacophony of color, naturalistic pictures of a smiling Nkrumah, of threatening lions, of King George VI, Queen Elizabeth and Prince Philip, of magical eyes and hands, birds, palm trees, and toads. Mammies also exploit and own the innumerable open "mammy-wagons," or "mammy-lorries," small open buses mounted on the chassis of prehistoric cars, which charge dangerously through the crowds. One could write a whole article about the mammy-wagons and their names, painted in big white letters on their creaking bodies: "Holy Boy," "Poor no one," "It pains you why?," "Never trust a woman," "Are you ready?," "Take me away, oh God," "Quo Vadis?" or "Not today." Accra loves powerful slogans. Nkrumah's party shouts, "Forward, never backward!' and the churches advertise "Powerful sermons."

Night life in Accra is frenzied. All night clubs, ranging from elegant to cheap, vibrate as in fever, but none compares to the Lido, alas now being modernized. The Lido is an open-air night club. Its owner, a greasy, broken-nosed Lebanese with a set of features which would frighten Al Capone, enjoys himself as much as his customers. Chewing what must be oversized chiclets he dances like an angel with the prettiest of future mammies, who flock to the Lido by the hundreds to perform their nearly religious dance rites. They are still slim and lissome, their small buttocks moving under long colorful skirts, their bodices smooth and tight, and their head-ties wound in jaunty bows. Dancing is no wild rock'n roll here, but is equally far removed from stuffy ballroom decorum. The dance is performed with intense abandon, close to a kind of trance, an ecstasy in which body and spirit become one. While dancing, no one talks, and even when the steps become wildly acrobatic the dance never degenerates into mere exhibitionism, but remains full of grace and control which comes from deep inside. The couples do not dance with each other, but dance toward each other in a unity of rapture, which does not just unite each couple, but enfolds all the couples, there under the stars, in a collective trance. A sea of couples moves in a savage rhythm, yet in prescribed orbits. There are no collisions except when a European couple, ridiculously rigid, self-consciously acrobatic, never forgetting themselves or the spectator, mix in. In the national dance, called "the Highlife," the rhythmic shuffle nearly dominates the music and the bodies sway intensively and subtly like a field of flowers.

During the day I had to inspect the inevitable hospitals, unavoidable chore on missions like mine. "This is our new sterilizing room . . . this is going to be our new male ward."—"Oh, yes . . . very interesting,"—"And this is our new air-conditioning plant, which will be connected next week."—"Marvelous! . . ." This does not mean that it is not all very impressive and that hard work is not being done and admirable progress made, but a hospital is just a hospital, except the one of Albert Schweitzer of course.

That week I also had to speak to the newly organized Ghana Medical Association which had a convention in Kumasi, the capital of the old Kingdom of Ashanti, a few hundred miles inland from Accra. It was a trip of several hours through the cocoa plantations which make up much of the wealth of Ghana. The doctors with whom I traveled did not know much about the country or else did not feel like talking except to boast about their fees, numbers of patients, and their own importance and influence, a professional deformity not limited to Ghana. But at the convention I noticed the same wonderful color blindness which is so striking everywhere in Ghana. African and European doctors mingled, completely oblivious to their own or other people's skin color. The convention took place in an enormous ultra-modern 500-bed hospital, which also houses an up-to-date school of nursing. However, the Kumasi Hospital had to be built carefully around a sacred tree, a monument of tremendous venerability where the Gold Throne, the Stool of Ashanti, descended from heaven. Close to it there was a hollow where until recently public executions were carried out. The Sacred Sword of Ashanti is also buried here with the handle sticking out of the earth. Legend has it that if this sword is pulled out of the ground Ashanti will perish. A skeptical doctor told me that in order to play it safe, however, concrete had been poured around it. The Ashantis, who still have their own ruler, the Asantehene, were an extraordinarily warlike tribe, which traditionally kept the coastal tribes as well as the Danes, Dutch, and British quite busy. At present they are often members of the Opposition Party, and keep Nkrumah busy.

After driving a few hours along the coast northward from Accra, I came to the charming, old-fashioned town of Cape Coast. There are still many colonial patrician houses, now occupied by African families. Cape Coast calls itself proudly "the Oxford of Ghana," and although there is no university, there are a number of primary and secondary schools. Like all the towns along the coast it has its castle. Ever since the fifteenth century, these castles, built by Portuguese, Dutch, Danish, and British colonizers, were fortified trading posts. Often the stones for the buildings came as ballast from Europe. Sailing away from Ghana no ballast was needed, for the ships were filled with slaves. "Christiansborg," in Accra, was such a slave castle, built by the Danes. Later it became the residence of the British Governor General. Now at last it is Nkrumah's palace. Justice on earth!

When I walked into Cape Coast's castle I heard homeric laughter coming from the higher floors. I was told that there were political prisoners above, for whom the castle had been reconditioned. They seemed to be having a good time. For the slaves it must have been very different. I opened a door marked "Dungeon," which gave access to the former slave warehouse. A broad vaulted passage led downward in a sweeping curve. It was dark, and when I struck a match, thousands of bats started up and tore like a storm past me down the passage. The steep floor was slippery and completely covered with bat dung. The walls were alive with thin-legged, eerie, transparent spiders waving long antennae. The air had a humid stench and I did not dare penetrate farther into the dungeon, the incline was too slippery and the atmosphere macabre, nightmarish. It was a relief to return to the courtyard and again hear the prisoners' gay songs. Looking down from the parapet, which was armed with antique cannons, I saw swarms of children playing on the beach and in the surf a hundred yards below.

"You are Dutch, aren't you?" asked my host, turning a white flash of a smile at me. "Well, from here your ancestors exported my people to the New World." "You are an Ashanti, aren't

Franck 7/59 Accra

you?" I replied. "Then you should know that your people lived from your slave trade nearly as much as from your gold." The slaves were mostly prisoners of war, but often villages were raided and burned just to choose the best merchandise among the inhabitants and kill the rest.

When I arrived in the nearby town of Elmina something queer was going on. Half a dozen mammy-wagons ("God the Killer" was among them) stormed at sixty miles an hour through the narrow main street. Pedestrians flattened themselves against house walls. The mammy-wagons were full of laughing and shouting Africans. Some of them were doing acrobatic tricks on the fenders. The wagons turned on two wheels around the church, sounding their horns continuously, and raced back. After a few moments they returned, swung again around the church, and started all over. The noise was deafening. In my panic I assumed that the whole town had gone berserk. Suddenly it was all finished and the vehicles stopped near the church. Their passengers were still laughing, their eyes wild with excitement. One of the drivers looked reasonably calm again and I asked him timidly what had been going on. "Oh," he said, "we celebrated a burial; one of the drivers died, poor fellow, we were just saying good-by to him." What I had witnessed in other words was a solemn funeral ceremony!

The young official at the airline office was all smiles. "I hear you were lecturing here, sir. . . . I want to study medicine in America, may I give you my card? I'll write to you, maybe you can find a place for me in a medical school." He weighed my luggage. "Oh my," he smiled, "you are terribly overweight. I'll have to charge you sixteen pounds. What a waste of money. Isn't it terrible? Would you be angry at me if I charged you five pounds, or do you think it is too much? It is such a shame to waste the money." Since this was the first time the profit had gone my way, I accepted shamefacedly. But, I tried to tell myself, that all the other times it had gone against me, as in the case of the old car I was offered by a government agency and for which I had to pay more than for any private car-hire ("No checks, please, cash only"). I hope I shan't hear from my airline friend.

In 1960 the population of Ghana was nearly 7 million, as compared to 4 million in 1948. The country is approximately 91,843 square miles in area (about the size of Oregon), with nearly 500,000 people living in its capital, Accra.

A traditional tension exists between the coastal Fanti tribe and the inland Ashanti tribe. The present inhabitants of Ghana are of fairly recent arrival (between the twelfth and seventeenth centuries).

About 30 per cent of the population is Christian, 10 per cent Moslem, and many animists.

The origin of the Ghanaians themselves is uncertain. The name Ghana (the former Gold Coast) was revived at the time of Independence on the assumption that its peoples were descendants of the Ghana Empire which existed in the Western Sudan more than a thousand years ago.

Along the coast, Portuguese, Dutch, Danish, German, and British traders built fortified castles as early as the fifteenth century. They were first used as trading posts for gold and slaves, until the slave trade was prohibited by the British in 1807. The Ghana slave trade was mostly in the hands of the warlike Kingdom of Ashanti, which fought a series of wars with the British until 1900, when the Ashantis were finally subdued. At this time the coastal area became a British crown colony, the remainder a protectorate.

In 1949, the then secretary of the United Gold Coast Convention, Dr. Kwame Nkrumah, formed his own "Convention People's Party." In 1951, after Nkrumah had served a prison term for sedition, his party scored a victory and he and his partisans became part of the new government. The African majority became active in policy-making. In 1954 the Gold Coast became practically self-governing. In 1957, when Ghana became independent, the new government prohibited parties based on racial, regional, or religious differences. The National Liberation Movement was reorganized to include the various opposition parties, and, known as the United Party, it has suffered severe persecution by the government since Independence. The new state consists of the old Gold Coast, the Ashanti Kingdom, the Northern Territories, and the Trust Territory of British Togoland. Ghana became a member of the British Commonwealth and on July 1, 1960, it declared itself a republic with Dr. Kwame Nkrumah as its chief of state. Since 1958 Ghana has signed treaties with the Republic of Guinea and the Republic of Mali, in order to form a Union with a view of becoming the nucleus for a future union of West African states.

The economy of Ghana is largely dependent upon the export of basic products, of which cocoa constitutes 60 per cent. Diamonds are another leading export. Ghana is the world's second largest producer of manganese, and in Ashanti there are large gold deposits of high quality. Although industrial output is low, the Volta River dam project, under construction, is expected to make possible the production of large quantities of aluminum from bauxite. Fishing and forestry are important activities. Cattle-raising, mainly concentrated in the North, is dependent on the control of sleeping sickness.

The educational system, started by British Christian missions, is now rapidly being taken over by the government. The two main institutions of higher learning are the University College of Ghana and Kumasi College of Technology, which are to be merged into the University of Ghana. The government and the Cocoa Marketing Board send thousands of Ghanaians abroad to study.

5 / Nigeria: Forge of Unity

"The Mainland Hotel?" asked my taxi driver at Lagos Airport. "Why the Mainland? Have you a reservation there?" "Isn't that the best hotel?" I asked in return. He looked around. His broad trustworthy ebony face smiled benignly, "It is the most expensive all right, sah, but I'll take you to the Island Hotel; it is newer, it is better, and it costs about half." He drove the long way from the airport, which is on the mainland, across the lagoon.

Lagos is an ant heap drowning in a lagoon. Four hundred thousand people thronged its maze of streets on both sides of interminable bridges choked with trucks, taxis, and all vintages of private cars. "This is our permanent traffic jam," the driver said, as we stood roasting for an hour or so like turkeys in a hot oven.

At last we entered Lagos proper, through narrow streets with milling crowds. The taxi nosed its way, and rounded corners into ever narrowing alleys. The driver had plenty of time to introduce himself as a cosmopolitan, a war veteran of Booma (Burma), Malaya, and Europe and a devout Catholic, only disguised in Moslem headgear, as well as a devoted father of multitudes of children. He stopped in front of a narrow passageway with a peeling sign, "Island Hotel." I picked my way between garbage cans and refuse to a stairway with another sign, "Island Hotel, second floor." When I reached the first floor and had read the scrawled obscenities on the dirty walls I

ended my explorations, descended, and announced forcefully, "Mainland Hotel, please." By the time we had crawled back across the bridge, the taxi meter had risen to astronomical figures. Typical greenhorn that I was, I had not understood that the Island Hotel probably belonged to a "brother" of my driver, which in Nigeria means just about everybody who belongs to your clan.

The Mainland apparently had a reservation and Dr. Fafunwa, a Nigerian with a New York University degree, was soon on hand to welcome me. It was Sunday and in the Mainland the *jeunesse dorée* of Lagos was having its fling. In the dining room serious German businessmen were eating their solitary dinners and British civil servants in khaki shorts were feeding their bony wives.

Large groups of Nigerian youths, uniformly fat and shiny and dressed in tentlike pieces of curtain material from Manchester mills, with little round caps jauntily perched on their round heads, were drinking Beaujolais, laughing noisily, and looking at everybody through superfluous sunglasses. The people of Lagos are a most attractive and fascinating lot, except those at the Mainland Hotel who look like overfed American suburbanites at a fancy-dress party.

I have drawn Lagos, so why describe it? But then, you can't draw the smells of the open sewers that run all through this city, where human life again seems to multiply like microbes in a frightening rhythm of fecundity. Along the waterfront are labyrinths of hovels, long scheduled for destruction but dearly beloved by generations of Yorubas who far prefer them to the neat little developments now laid out on the Mainland far from their native Marina, which smells like a garbage heap but brings ecstasy to the eye. Yes, it is of overwhelming beauty, for from this garbage heap spring multitudes of human beings full of vitality, spouting intelligence out of shining eyes. There are children of such openness and charm that one would cuddle them all day long, young women of such beauty with their flowering peachlike skins, and youths with such live bodies and graceful movements that enchantment wins immediately over initial disgust and fear.

As everywhere in Africa I immediately felt safe with these people. Of course during a sudden outburst of organized or exasperated hostility mobs anywhere on earth are redoubtable. But normally it takes only a smile here to get a response, and a sign of simple humanity, a bit of humor, is enough to make friends. Around the Oba's palace (the Oba is the ancient hereditary king) the labyrinth of tiny streets seems alive with crowds until deep into the night. Parties are flowering around tiny oil lamps which blow walls of smoke around each expanding gathering. The lagoon shines in fairy-tale reflections. Ghosts of fishing nets form filigreed walls along the bumpy roads with their bejeweled puddles.

In the morning the Marina is transformed into an endless market. Fish is constantly thrown from pointed boats. Firewood is sold in tiny bundles by solemn patriarchs. In the middle of the crowds, minuscule restaurants suddenly appear, where women cook yams and serve them from improvised snack bars of inverted boxes. At the yam market nearby these big, unwieldy, starchy roots are sold by the thousands, although each eager saleswoman has only a few. Coolies are removing sand from barges in immense, heavily loaded baskets, which they carry on their heads; their black bodies are spotted with mud in abstract expressionist designs. In front of a record stall youngsters are jitterbugging wildly to the music, trucks missing them by magic.

At a juju stand (juju is the aboriginal magic) the crazy-eyed owner asked me suspiciously, "Are you South African?" and became friendly when I assured him that I was not. His wares did not look very attractive, indispensable as they are if you want to put curses on your neighbors, compelling them to die quickly or to love you hotly. He had a fine collection of dried corpses of rats, monkey skulls in all sizes, and a freshly killed huge cat's head, whose glassy eyes fixed me with a chilling stare. The juju vendor's eyes were not much less frightening, clearly a *déformation professionnelle.* He showed me a magic plant to which a chameleon was tied. A boy, with a pitiful little bird in his hand ("I am trying to train it," he said) was experimenting with the mutual reactions of bird and chameleon.

"What do you think of all this business?" I asked the boy with the bird. "I am a Christian," he said defensively. "To me all this is nonsense." The witch doctor went on in his ecclesiastical drone explaining the uses of the bat skulls, the mice skulls, the jawbones, the pins and needles to be lethally stuck through images, the cowrie shells to be given, ground in water, to babies with mouth infections. To him these things were all holy, potent objects, and he tried to explain them to me, an American, who was not a South African. From the leaves of another plant one could make a concoction, which, smeared on the eyes, would give visions of things far away. The chameleon's plant had the special faculty to change your personality the way a chameleon can change his colors. The Christian schoolboy was

still smirking, but the witch doctor did not seem to mind. "I am a Car-thlic," the boy repeated proudly in a pure Nigerian Dublin brogue.

At the goat market the touching, gentle creatures quietly, patiently, waited in the merciless sun for a buyer; one newborn lamb floated dead in the open sewer. A fat, blue-gowned Moslem accosted me and insisted on selling me a goat, at which I must have glanced tenderly. "Sorry," I said, "but I still have to travel all over Africa." "She gentle," he said with a smile. "I travel by plane," I smiled back. "But you can take on your lap," he tried to convince me. "A bit difficult with feeding," I bowed. "Oh, no," he objected, "I'm give you big bag of hay with it, free!" It all happened with so many polite smiles from both sides that I'll never know who had been kidding whom, for we were still smiling and bowing to each other when we shook hands and went our ways.

Lagos is a blue city. The Yorubas dress in all its shades. Their women, stately and proud, are swathed in cerulean skirts, cobalt blouses, ultramarine scarves, indigo head-ties in all combinations and patterns, and always in contrast to the deep mahogany of their radiant faces. One has the feeling that these great females dominate the city and tie it to the earth triumphantly. The men, on the other hand, riding their bicycles in their blowing curtain robes or chattering in amorphous groups, seem incidental extras without substantial weight. Yet they have their function: of every ten children five still die in early childhood and Yorubas like to count children by the dozen.

Dr. Fafunwa, the Nigerian, could not help showing me all this, but he was anxious for me to see the new Lagos too, not only the traditional ant heap. He lives with his Vermont wife in a neat suburban house close to the new developments, African shades of Levittown, of which I suppose one must be

proud, for as a witty Frenchman said, "The picturesque is the discomfort of others." Fafunwa was born in the Marina, but he has outgrown it and his children will never experience life there.

I had to look at the big new government buildings and the Federal Parliament, outdoing each other in "airport-modern" style. Houses on the old streets had been bulldozed down to make space for wide avenues and for the immense parking lot for the new cars, three hundred of them, from Jaguar limousines through Fords and Chevrolets to Volkswagens, all lacquered green and yellow, the national colors, for the Independence celebrations. "A waste of money of course," every Nigerian tells you. But a waste of money to be proud of, and "maybe after the celebrations one could pick up a Jaguar for a song!"

Past the parking lot, past the huge new hotel, past the enormous blocks of modern apartments to be used by the parliamentary delegates and their polygamous families during Parliament sessions in Lagos, we drove to the forbidding beach with its treacherous surf where swimming is suicide. In the little compounds on the wide, white beach, small sects with their fanatical adherents were in action. A lone black figure in a white robe stood erect, his arms outstretched, in front of a tiny hut—the Church of Jesus the Second. A little farther the "Cherubim and Seraphim" were lying on their bellies in the sand, and a bearded priest, a rough cross in his outstretched hand, was bellowing a sermon at them. In the distance two men carried a huge black pig, suspended from a wooden pole by its tied legs, writhing and shrieking louder than the surf and the hymn-singers.

We walked back to the hotel, across markets so crowded that the dirty ground was nowhere to be seen. Chickens and ducks slipped between our legs, children sold food in rolled banana leaves, men peddled gaudy cushions piled in improbable columns on their heads. We passed the skyscraper of a new maternity hospital where blue Yoruba women crowded around newborn babies and curtsied to the young mothers. We jumped over stinking sewers, admired the signs, "Keep Lagos clean," on large billboards, and walked around the men peeing against the supports.

In the falling dusk the market women before the hotel had lighted their oil lamps. Some of their customers carried burning storm lamps in enamel basins on their heads. The peddlers of wrist watches and ball-point pens blocked our way. The cripples in front of the hotel shouted, "Evening, sah," and fought over tips, angrily going at each other with their withered legs and mutilated arm stumps. From the balcony of the dining room my eye swept once more over the lagoon, now delicately pink and purple, serene and quiet, with a thousand lights flickering in the ant heap beyond. . . .

The Airport of Lagos looked as if a mass exodus were taking place. It was black, very black, with black people, yet there was only one plane, a Britannia turbo-prop, standing ready to fly to Kano and beyond, to England. It was no exodus, however, just a politician going on "home leave," being seen off by his whole constituency in festive dress. "Home leave" is unfortunately finished now that Nigeria is independent. It is the end of a wonderful joke. Since British officials were given home leave every two years and Nigerians were on equal footing with them, they were given home leave too and this was their chance for a free trip to "U.K." I may well have witnessed the last Nigerian going "home"; from now on "home" is where their heart is supposed to be.

Kano, photographed from the right angle, is pure *Arabian Nights,* but it depends on the angle. For Kano has many faces. It still shows its English colonial face around the huge sprawling compound of the mediocre hotel, at the enormous airport where for local color an old Hausa on his white camel announces arrivals and departures by blowing his six-foot museum trumpet. From another angle Kano is the rambling outer city of nonde-

script avenues and boundless markets where "foreigners" live, "foreigners" being non-Northerners, the Ibos from the East and the Yorubas from the West, who, whether Moslem or not, are never integrated into the authentic life of Kano. They are not allowed to live in the old city which, ringed with dilapidated ramparts, is still accessible through twelve gates. They can no longer be closed, but still they represent the old orthodox Moslem bastion resisting defilement.

The center of the old city is the Emir's Palace facing the huge new mosque. I caught old Kano's spirit when, looking down from the minaret which dominates the ancient quarter, I heard three trumpet blasts and saw, deep below, the massive doors of the palace swing open. Preceded by a jeep full of Kelly-green-and-red-robed bodyguards and by white figures on horseback, a black Rolls-Royce crawled with exasperating slowness across the ocher expanse of the main square. The trumpet flourishes continued and I discovered that they were coming from the horn of the Rolls. Then suddenly the whole labyrinth awakened to life. Tiny figures in white and pale blue robes seemed to spring from every corner of the old city and to run to the square, answering the trumpets with a concert of animal roars. They all ran to watch the Rolls-Royce pass, greeting it while still far away, raising the right arm and closed fist in homage as if in mock Communist salute. Then, as the Emir passed, they bowed deep into the dust. The young Yoruba who had guided me up the minaret, spat on the floor and sneered: "That is independent Nigeria for you!" Later he took me to the Emir's Court in front of the Palace, where I saw a man being dragged to face his judge, the Emir, and kicked to his knees by the guards when he refused to kneel. The Yoruba growled: "That man is a political prisoner. I am a Moslem, too, but the time will come when we will kick the Emir to the ground." True, there is opposition to the almost absolute power of the emirs in the North, but it will be quite a long time before they are kicked to the ground. The enlightened Moslem rulers like the Sardauna of Sokoto may well have to bend a bit, however, in order not to be broken.

"The British," my guide said bitterly, "with their 'indirect' rule gave all the power to the emirs; British rule would have been preferable. The British at least were fair and decent, the emirs are not."

The court session we were looking at in front of the palace, although enraging my friend, was a rare delight to the artist drawing it. Around the Emir, like a mass of fairy-tale figures, his courtiers were squatting on the ground, their bodies covered with great silky robes, their immobile black sculptured faces peering out from under huge turbans. The Emir's bodyguards, huge fellows with frightening faces, kept the populace at a respectful distance, while runners brought messages from prison and palace to the Emir. The Emir's horse, with its silver saddle, its reins adorned with triangular leather pennants, was patiently waiting behind him. A poor crippled wreck of a woman came crawling on all fours from the prison to the court. She was somehow involved, I understood, in the mysterious disappearance of a child. After short questioning she crawled back across the huge, dusty square to her cell. The bodyguards were not cruel to her, merely indifferent, their faces distant and unseeing. A female prison guard followed her at a distance, as if to avoid contamination. After the court session was over the dignitaries strolled across the square between the palace and the offices, bowing to each other and stopping for a bit of polite chitchat until, jumping into their silver-adorned saddles, they rode back to their villages.

Besides all this pomp there is the world of the cripples. Kano seems to be filled with them. They are crawling on all fours, hopping on one leg or on none. Their arms are twisted like olive branches, their legs swollen by elephantiasis. The lepers drag themselves along on their stumps; the sufferers from yaws look at you out of faces without noses, without ears, without eyes. Kano has an orthopedic hospital, but since Allah sends suffering who goes there? And how many can it help or rehabilitate anyway?

Every fifth person you meet is blind and is led by a begging child, but who gives? The eye hospital is of little help, because trachoma and common eye infections are too long neglected by the people. Hence this appalling incidence of blindness. But to these people blindness and all other physical illnesses are not tragedy but simply fate, almost indifferently accepted.

Whatever there is to relieve this suffering—medical services, hospitals—has been built and organized by Europeans. It is unfair to say that the interference of European power has always been to the detriment of the African population. This seems a sentimental notion probably caused by guilt feelings for past colonial misdeeds or shortcomings, which are now regretted. Why daren't we realize that when the history of Africa is reviewed after the period of turbulence through which we are now going, it may well be agreed that the much maligned colonization was the catalyst which activated the stagnant cultural history of Africa? The Sleeping Beauty possibly needed a forceful kiss to awaken her from her millennial sleep.

Seen from the large rocky Dalla Hill within the walled city, Kano looks like a tortuous puzzle of russet cardboard; every house is surrounded by walls, which in turn are enclosed by more walls. The houses are topped by strange ornamental structures looking like donkey's ears, which no one could explain. The mud walls are often carved with intricate geometric designs. Going into a house through a low door which is usually the only source of light and air, one enters room after clay-floored room with sparse low pieces of furniture. Even the very rich live in these dark caves without comfort or sanitary installations. A doctor told me that he had visited the richest man of Kano, perhaps wealthier even than the Emir, and found the old man dying in such a house, on a dirty bed in an airless room lighted only by a smoky oil lamp.

Riding in my rented old Morris through the center of the old city, I was greeted by shouts of "Congo, Congo," which did not sound too violent, but which I did not like in a city where the whole day I had not met another white man. On a lonely road on the outskirts the car suddenly stalled. We had run out of gas. The driver, who did not speak a word of English, gestured what had happened and went to look for gas. We were standing in front of a house where children were huddled in the shade, holding large wooden slabs on which Koran texts were written; an old teacher was instructing them. From the doorway a man with a haughty Hausa face scowled at me. I began to draw the scene, first making sure that the car doors were locked. Tall, thin, high-breasted Fulani women in indigo rags peered into the car impassively, balancing calabashes of water on their heads. It was as unbearably hot as it only can get in a parked car under the tropical sun and I was drawing as in a nightmare, badly, just in order not to go mad. The next service station was probably miles away. The man in the doorway seemed to fix me more aggres- sively. I closed the windows of my oven nearly all the way and continued to scribble. Suddenly I stiffened as a horrifying growl arose next to my ear. I swung around and looked into monstrous white eyes. "A rabid dog," my first shock said, while I burned my fingers on the handle of the window I tried to close. But it was not a dog. Mean-looking emaciated men were holding a blind hyena by a chain and had forced the monster against the car window. They were shouting and grimacing. A man farther down the road was dragging a smaller hyena through the dust, the stretched neck of the creature tensed to the breaking point. I was stunned with horror, for I did not realize that these were simply beggars shouting for pennies. From the opposite window a little girl leered seductively at me. She obviously belonged to my visitors and was the cashier. Her eyes were lined with poisonous green make-up, her lower lip painted violent carmine, making her look like an old prostitute. She held out her hand

and just as I hurried to buy her off with a few pennies, she thrust the head of a hissing python into the window as an encore. The animals and the humans who shared their misery and humiliation then disappeared down the dusty road. In the trembling heat it seemed as if they danced away in a desperate pavan.

By the time my heart rate had become normal and I tried again to draw, my driver came trotting back, a radiant smile on his face and a quart of gasoline in a bottle. I shook my head when he started the motor and gestured, "No, get more gasoline!" He grinned and said, "Yes, sah," and pushed the starter. I got out and gestured violently, "Turn around!" He shouted, "Yes, sah," but obviously thought I had gone mad.

The trouble with Africa is that all Africans have been taught to say "Yes, sah" or "Oui, monsieur" without having any idea what you are talking about. I did not feel like walking back through Kano and having to assume personal responsibility for the Congo situation. So I decided to cook in my oven until an English-speaking person came along. Two minutes later the miracle happened: around the corner suddenly appeared a little truck with an African driver in new dark blue overalls and a peaked cap with the magic inscription: "Esso." "Do you speak English?" I shouted. The driver shouted back; "Yes, sah," and followed up with, "Anything I can do for you, sah?" "You can indeed," I said, "I am sitting here drawing because we ran out of gas. And with hyenas and all that, you see . . ." "I'll be right back, sah," the man said, repeating the same in Hausa to my driver. Soon afterward he appeared with two cans of gasoline. The old Morris shot forward to the hotel.

Kano Market is famous all over Nigeria. Peasants and craftsmen from hundreds of miles around come there to sell and to buy. The market is a labyrinth in which you are lost before you have walked two hundred yards. You are lost between a thousand tiny stalls selling plastic junk, silver-adorned saddles, Hausa swords, juju skulls, handwoven camel blankets, indigo cloth, gold damask cloaks, dungarees, silver ankle bands, and what not. The Hausas, usually so proud and inaccessible, shout jovially from stall to stall; they look savagely threatening when you offer too little, but calm down again when you increase your bid, and even help you to get out of the maze, where they could so easily have made mincemeat or at any rate "medicine" out of you.

The cattle market on the outskirts of the town is a vast plain, where the sun beats down. The lowing zebus are standing around, and camels with their ungainly hunchbacked bodies are tottering on thin legs with flat feet. On their snakelike necks swing monstrous skulls from which their disenchanted eyes size you up arrogantly. Donkeys and horses, one foreleg bound up with rope, limp around on the dry grass. Cows are bound to each other to prevent their straying. Vultures noiselessly search the ground hopefully and hundreds of sparrows are living symbiotically off the insect fauna on the backs of the cows. A sick ox, unable to shake the birds off, covered with them as a carcass with flies, is periodically rescued by a boy on a bicycle, whose robe flutters wildly in the hot wind. Sometimes a prospective buyer comes galloping along proudly on his horse. The cattle dealers get up from under their large black umbrellas and the haggling begins, interrupted by blind men led by begging boys. A woman carries a huge load of firewood in a bundle on her back, held by a leather band across her forehead. In front of her she holds a baby on outstretched arms, as if offering it to a cruel god.

I flew to Enugu, capital of the Eastern Region. Enugu is an artificial town because the Ibos are an agricultural people, not city builders like the Yorubas; it is not too long ago that they

offered human sacrifices to the yam gods. Since their national dress was the nude skin, there is very little else in the way of native costume. People walk around in all combinations of European clothing between neat rows of semi-detached cement-block houses along sloping streets. The lush hilly countryside around the city looks like central France under a steaming tropical sky.

I was met at the airport by an Indian doctor who had been an anesthetist in Enugu for years and who introduced me to the hospital of which he was rightly proud. Most of the doctors at this hospital, and all the specialists, were Ibos who had studied in England. Only recently have Nigerians begun to come to America also to study, and respect for American education is growing. The older Nigerian doctors still have the strange

Franck VIII '60

notion that in America you simply buy your medical degree for five hundred dollars, the way you can buy a Doctor of Divinity degree in Liberia if you still have a few traveler's checks left. Speaking of traveler's checks I had occasion to change one at the local bank. Two fellow customers asked me if they might have a look at them. I explained the use of traveler's checks, which they thought a brilliant invention, and then one of my new friends pointed to the Roman soldier who, for some unknown reason, adorns the American Express Company's checks. "Is that the King of America?" the gaunt white-robed Hausa boy on my left asked, but the Ibo in his sport shirt on my right laughed in his face and said: "Stupid, don't you know that America has no king? That must be President Eisenhower."

While we were walking through the hospital, the Indian doctor introduced me to the huge African surgeon, who said, "There is an American film tonight, and we were going to look at it. Would you join us? We can have a drink afterward. It might interest you to see one of your national products in African context." The Indian doctor added, "People don't go much for American films around here, our Indian films are much more popular. I wonder when finally somebody will get the bright idea of making African films for Africans, with African actors, who mean something to the people. You Americans are probably waiting for the Russians to do it!" And so, in the dark open-air theater under the stars of Enugu, I had to suffer through a film with Miss Monroe wiggling her hips and coyly uncovering what African women let dangle so unconcernedly over their soup pots and their babies. To watch Miss Monroe being thrown around by six effeminate boys in white bowler hats on a mock stage complete with a standardized cigar-chewing Broadway producer is an exotic experience in Africa. The music, an insipid cloying tune, was obsessively repeated. Then duets followed between Miss Monroe and a moronically crooning individual who was moving his hips in weak imitation of what any octogenarian African can do ever so much better. It made me wonder what went on in these African heads in Enugu. Staring at the incomprehensible erotic rituals of a bogus New York night club, the Africans, for whom sex is something simple and natural were probably completely baffled. When it was over the African surgeon said contemptuously, in his most perfect Oxford accent; "So this is America, is it, and not even a gangster in it as in all your other films! I say, charming country, charming country. . . ."

As so often in Africa, I tried again desperately to correct stereotyped pictures of life in America. But who am I to fight this pernicious myth? For years we have exported a mythical image of America, manufactured in Hollywood and on Madison Avenue, which has made the world both envious and contemptuous. It is the image of a land of superficial morons and phonies, swimming in glamour, luxury, and waste, and solving all life problems by the conventional violence of gun and knockout. Shall we ever be able to redeem this damage and represent ourselves as a human community, moved by the adult emotions and aspirations we have in common with all mankind? I do not envy Mr. Gordon, the cultivated American Negro directing the U.S. Information office in Enugu, who is trying to present a more realistic picture of America.

The trip from Enugu to Onitsha takes two hours, driving African style. This means that, trusting to your invulnerability, you screech at top speed around the curves of the hills beyond Enugu, whirl through villages hidden in insular groves of trees with cassava, Guinea corn, and yam crops stored around the huts, tear through monotonous tunnels of virgin forest or jungle swamps, and creak over chains of bridges spanning gulleys

choked with vegetation. You fly nonchalantly into villages with odd two-storied houses which look like windowless caricatures of nineteenth-century European respectability, pass a community house, a baby clinic, an Anglican mission (being nothing but a straw-hut compound), an imitation Westminster cathedral of corrugated iron and mud brick, a mud hut with a grandiose sign "Royal Hotel."

In every tiny hamlet you flash through there are "photo studios" with elaborate names (everybody with a box camera must set himself up as a professional photographer). Emaciated dogs are run over gleefully by crazy mammy-wagons bearing their inimitable inscriptions, "Charity begins with Prosperity," "Live and let live," "Wisdom before Action." And everywhere along the road there is the never-ending procession of women, erect as majesties, carrying in enamel washbasins their harvests, their meals, and their implements. Their babies bob along in

scarlet slings on their backs, and their tiny tots run at their sides balancing machetes as large as themselves on their kinky elongated skulls.

Everywhere are schools, as though the whole population of Nigeria from cradle to grave had no greater wish than to go to school, any school. Suddenly there is a detour and, slithering over a red mud track, through puddles and over logs, we are thrown back without warning into eternal Africa. Struggling through the mud we get back to the main road and continue our race to Onitsha.

At Onitsha glistens the Niger, that huge mysterious river for centuries uncharted, now placid and like an immense lake whose other bank disappears toward the horizon. The river, seen across terraced meadows which calmly descend to its edge, is filled with sleepy craft. But suddenly, after crossing quiet suburbs, I am sucked into the tumultuous scene of Onitsha itself with its vast, permanent market, the greatest covered market of all Nigeria, where everything can be bought whether it is legitimately salable or not: oil lamps made of old tins, diamonds, red peppers, stolen tractor motors, and what not. There had just been a raid in which hundreds of traders had been arrested because they had sold antibiotics, barbiturates, and all kinds of dangerous drugs over and under the counter. Penicillin shots against venereal diseases are given on street corners through a man's trousers into his buttocks. Long sheds are filled to the last corner with piles of textiles, leather goods, tools and instruments of all kinds, cosmetics, and chromium-plated bicycles. Part of the market along the river is built on an ever expanding garbage heap, which smells to high heaven.

In majestic concrete steps the market descends to the river, where long straw-covered houseboats crawl with human and animal life. The dugouts on the river have straw mats for sails;

the oarsman sits aft on a carved, elevated, little stool. Midships over small open fires the women cook the meals.

My African hotel was a caricature of a European one, or rather the European tradition was already overgrown by African neglect. The mahogany furniture was scratched and dilapidated, the lavatory out of order, the menus soup-stained, the food inedible. I left the hotel early in the morning without regret and a little itchy, for the mosquito nets had been full of holes. Also, before boarding the ferry to cross the Niger, the wide boundary between Eastern and Western Nigeria, I just had to see that market again.

On the steps in the white morning light thousands of women, their children around them, were sitting in clusters, patiently displaying their wares in shallow baskets: an eggplant, some cassavas, neat little piles of ten groundnuts, five vermilion peppers, six small cones of native peanut butter, or tiny wet heaps of "bitter herb" looking like spoonfuls of spinach. Each of them being an eager part of this surging social life, they were chattering and haggling, shouting and laughing in the ever fascinating human contact which can be had by anyone who has two yams, three cigarettes, or a chicken to sell.

Arrived at the big ferryboat, the last mammy-wagon could just be squeezed in between all the trucks and tank cars and jalopies. An old blind porter, skin-over-bones, his white eyes staring into the sun, sweat streaming down his black face, followed me aboard, carrying my big, heavy case of drawings on his head. When I wanted to give him a shilling a white man stopped me. "Not more than threepence," he warned. Well-tailored students, market women with fish, old-school-tied lawyers crowded the ferry, which sometimes nearly collided with the dugouts coming downstream. Seen from mid-river, Onitsha, with its Anglican-looking churches, seemed to change into a placid English country

town as, on the other side, the village of Asaba began to emerge as a cluster of huts-on-stilts, built around another English-looking rural church. From the steep muddy bank convoys of trucks seemed to hang precariously, as if ready to fall onto the trembling ferry.

I was not very quiet in my mind, because I had arranged for another driver to pick me up at Asaba. He was not at the ferry. "Maybe at the Rest House," somebody suggested. The Rest House, on top of the hill, was an old colonial building, clean and whitewashed like a monastery, its ground sloping down in green velvet steps to the Niger; the African manager was suave as a Riviera maître d'hôtel. Luckily here Wahabi, my new driver, was waiting. I never got to know to what tribe he really belonged, for he did not speak a word of English, except once when our car had broken down toward evening in an uncomfortable jungle, he surprised me with, "Car dead!" His young jet-black face was nobly Roman and delicately carved with those

tribal marks which to the insider are like a passport, for they denote both tribe and place of birth. A few generations ago this might mean protection in friendly territory or absolute doom if spotted by an enemy. After Wahabi set my Volkswagen in motion, he became one with it. In many hours of driving he never turned his head even one degree. When I offered him peppermints I had to put them in his mouth, because he did not take his hands off the wheel. When I motioned "faster," he would fly ahead with absolute surety, take sharp corners as by magic, dodge crazy buses as if anticipating their antics. There has never been a driver like Wahabi. For twelve hours he was car. That evening, the minute he stopped, he immediately collapsed into deep sleep and I could not arouse him to get him into bed. The next morning we left for Benin City—but let me quote an earlier traveler:

As we neared Benin City we passed several human sacrifices, live women slaves gagged and pegged on their backs to the ground, the abdominal wall being cut in the form of a cross, and the uninjured gut hanging out. These poor women were allowed to die like this in the sun. Men slaves, with their hands tied at the back and feet lashed together, also gagged, were lying about. As we neared the city, sacrificed human beings were lying in the path and bush—even in the king's compound the sight and stench of them was awful. Dead and mutilated bodies were everywhere—by God! May I never see such sights again! . . .

In the King's Compound, on a raised platform or altar, beautiful idols were found. All of them were caked over with human blood. Lying about were big bronze heads, dozens in a row, with holes at the top, in which immense carved ivory tusks were fixed. One can form no idea of the impression it made on us. The whole place reeked of blood. Fresh blood was dripping off the figures and altars (months afterwards, when we broke up these long altars, we found that they contained human bones). . . .

In front of the King's Compound is an immense wall . . . and at each end are two big juju trees. In front, stakes have been driven into the ground, and cross-pieces of wood lashed to them. On this frame-work live human beings are tied to die of thirst and heat, and ultimately to be dried by the sun and eaten by the carrion birds. . . .

There were two bodies on the first tree and one on the other. At the base of them the whole ground was strewn with human bones and decomposing bodies, with their heads off. Two looked like white men . . . the flesh was off their hands and feet, and the heads had been cut off and removed. . . . All along the road, too, more decapitated bodies were found, blown out by the heat of the sun; the sight was sickening. . . .

—*Great Benin*
Diary of a surgeon, by H. Ling Roth, 1897.

The official report of the British Foreign Office (No. 6, 1897) relates:

The city presented the most appalling sight, particularly around the King's quarters, from which four large main roads lead to the compounds of the bigger chiefs, the city being very scattered. Sacrificial trees in the open spaces still held the corpses of the latest victims—seven in all were counted—and on every path a freshly sacrificed corpse was found lying, apparently placed there to prevent pursuit. One large open space, 200 to 300 yards in length, was strewn with human bones and bodies in all stages of decomposition. Within the walls the sight was, if possible, more terrible. Seven large sacrifice compounds were found inclosed by walls . . . against the end wall in each, under a roof was raised a dais with an earthen sacrificial altar. . . . The altars were covered with streams of dried human blood and the stench was too frightful. It would seem that the populace sat around in these huge compounds while the Juju priests performed the sacrifices for their edification. In the various sacrifice compounds were found open pits filled with human bodies. . . . In one of the pits, partially under other bodies, was found a victim, still living. . . .

In the outlying parts of the city the same sights were met and the annual expenditure of human life in sacrifice must have been enormous. Most of the wells were also found filled with human bodies. . . .

The man who wrote the first report did not come by Volkswagen. He was the doctor of a British punitive expedition which was sent to end the horrors of human sacrifices, barely a lifetime ago.

I have long been fascinated by Benin, the "City of Blood," because of its fantastically beautiful bronze sculptures, which are, together with those of Ife, the noblest of Africa. We now look upon these Benin bronzes merely as art, forgetting that with all the sophistication of the cire-perdue process they really have to be seen as part of a bloodthirsty cult and imagined to be caked with layers of coagulated human blood.

I drove into the "City of Blood" through gay markets and past modern schools with children playing exuberantly on green playgrounds, past the Oil Palm Research Institute which is doing so much to improve the quality of palm culture in the country, and finally arrived at the Police Station to ask where I could lunch. A sleepy sergeant kindly pointed the way to the local Catering Rest House. My grandfather in his day would probably have been differently received! The streets were thronged with festive people and traffic was held up by at least six different processions of wildly dancing Africans in their Sunday best. There was a peculiar quality to their excitement and drumming and their fixed stares. There was something provocative in their laughter, that ominous rumble from deep in the throat which can make African laughter bloodcurdling. A few times the car was stopped by the dancing crowds and instinctively I turned up windows and locked doors, for with all the gaiety something malignant seemed to smolder between the rival dancing groups which filled the streets. I had experienced this only in films like *Orpheo Negro* or the carnival scene in *Les Enfants du Paradis*.

At the Catering Rest House no one took notice of me. The parking lot was filled with large American cars flying ministerial pennants or the flag of the Action Group, one of the political parties: a green palm tree on white. Here too the place had a carnival atmosphere, but the laughter was triumphant and the figures merely grotesque. Lounge and dining room were filled with people dressed with such extravagance as can be seen only in Africa. Apparently all the tumult was about an election in which Awolowo's Action Group had triumphed. The victory was being celebrated by politicians and ministers and their immensely fat wives, bedecked with yards of spectrum-colored cloth. One bellowing minister, drunk with victory and beer, a bullet-round, two-hundred-pounder wearing a white tentlike wrap and something like a chef's white hat, was distributing cigars all over. With him, in a purple damask tunic draped over striped trousers and patent leather pumps, a tall asparagus of a chief with a huge golden crown over his shrunken black face was pumping the hand of another bigwig, a solemn man in a magenta silk toga and a boater. Out of the dining room came a man in sunglasses and evening dress, a Boy Scout's whistle around his neck. A short fat man in a dinner jacket and a purple skirt, a fez on his head, violently elbowed his way through the crowd, trying to find an empty chair.

Discovering a phone in a corner of the lobby, I decided to call the Oba's Palace, for I felt I absolutely must meet the grandson of the man who had been banished by the British in 1897 because he had people so picturesquely sacrificed if they as much as sneezed at the wrong moment. But as I was about to lift the receiver it was grabbed by the fat beringed fingers of a bizarre man, a fat albino with red hair and a pink Negroid face. Dressed in pin-striped suit and bowler, he looked as if he had stepped out of a London fashion magazine. The waiters treated him with great respect and I was told that he was a powerful

March VIII 67 E. Nigeria

politician. After he had bellowed into the telephone in Afro-English, he walked imperiously to the lounge, swinging his walking stick as in a vaudeville act, and switched on the radio. The next second the whole phantasmagoria became immersed in the *"Ode to Joy"* from Beethoven's Ninth Symphony: *"Seid umschlungen, Millionen . . ."*

I finally got the Oba's Palace on the phone. "This is Mr. Izak speaking," a cultured African voice answered. "May I speak to the Oba's secretary, please?" "I am the Oba's secretary." "I am just passing through Benin," I said. "I am an American writer and artist and I should very much like to pay my respects to His Highness before leaving Benin." Mr. Izak apparently consulted the Oba, for after a few minutes I had my appointment.

There was a gate in the thick ocher mud wall which, about a mile long, enclosed the palace compound. Entering the gate I found myself in a large bare rectangular courtyard baking in the sun. A sprawling one-story building occupied the entire far end of the area. A sentry sauntered slowly toward me, his rifle slung over his shoulder. "I have an appointment with the Oba," I said. "Would you notify Mr. Izak, please?"

Some time passed. A bit to the left of the center of the courtyard was a small pavilion, open on all sides, containing a low altar on which a frightful sculptured idol was standing, arms extended. Strange ritual implements were lying on the awesome altar. A voice from somewhere shouted, "Don't go near." Small nude children were playing hide-and-seek around the blood-thirsty-looking god.

The door to the palace opened and out came a youth of about eighteen, nude except for white briefs, powerfully built and with a face exactly like one of the bronze heads from the Ife Museum. He seemed to be waiting for me. "May I speak to Mr. Izak, please?" I asked. "I am Mr. Izak," he said. "Will you come in?"

The door, heavy and studded with iron nails like that of a medieval fortress, clanked shut behind me as, a little ill at ease, I followed Mr. Izak. He led me into a long, low room, lighted only by a skylightlike hole in the roof. Behind a big desk sat a man in a white robe and skull cap. His dark ascetic face reminded me of Nehru. His intelligent eyes looked at me through gold-rimmed glasses. He got up to shake hands with me.

The walls of the room were covered with photographs which I felt it was impolite to study too closely. I could just make out that they were photographs of royal British visits and festive occasions in the old barbaric days.

"Sit down," the Oba said, pointing to a very deep, old armchair from which I thought I'd never be able to get up. Mr. Izak noiselessly retreated to a dark corner and at a sign from the Oba brought me a quart of ice-cold beer. "Tell me," the Oba started the conversation, looking at me searchingly, "you are an American, aren't you?" I nodded. "Now could you, please, in a few words tell me the precise difference between the Democratic and Republican parties?"

The audience lasted three-quarters of an hour, and while I drank too much beer the Oba showed me one of his prize possessions: a book about Negro life in the United States. It was printed in the thirties and the pictures of the sharecroppers, the Ku Klux Klan, and the lynchings were not pretty. We were interrupted only by many little tots entering unceremoniously but noiselessly who were given pennies by the ruler. At last Mr. Izak, who had sat motionless in his corner, opened the great door again for me and I found myself dazed but undamaged on the inner court, the same court where Dr. Roth in 1897 had seen hundreds of dead and dying, "gagged and pegged humans." Mr. Izak's idol-like face was shining in an obsequious smile and I somehow felt that it would not be out of place to offer him a

week VIII 60 moslems at prayer

Ife, a name known to all art lovers in the world, is an uninteresting town with low buildings, all russet walls and corrugated roofs. But in its middle there is the Museum, a white modern building which looks like a civic center in Westchester. There is a permanent exhibition of the amazing sculptures of Ife, discovered some fifty years ago by Frobenius and remaining ever since one of the great marvels and enigmas of the world of art. No two archeologists ever agreed on either the makers or the dates of the amazingly naturalistic and yet nobly classical bronze heads which may date from the fourteenth to the sixteenth century. This mysterious art flourished and suddenly disappeared in one of those miraculous outbursts of creativity which made painting flower for a short period in seventeenth-century Netherlands or classical music in Vienna around the turn of the nineteenth century.

Apart from the bronze heads there are terra-cotta figures showing gagged persons prepared for sacrifice and human figures with all kind of pathological deformities like elephantiasis, the significance of which is not known. Yet, Ife being the cradle of the Yoruba tribe—and according to the Yoruba religion the birthplace of the world—the meaning of its art must have been essentially religious, because traditionally for the Yoruba every event from his birth to his death was pervaded and regulated by religion. It struck me that in Ife I found the first hint of a smile I ever saw in African sculpture.

I could have written much more about Ife, if one of its many gods had not caught up with me. I had started to draw in the Law Court, a huge open shed in which every door and pillar was adorned with witty and sometimes cruel totem-pole-like carvings. But I could not stand very long the burning sun roasting my neck. Exasperated I grabbed my camera to take a quick snapshot of a particularly sarcastic-looking idol. I stepped back to

shilling for his trouble. Hardly had he pocketed it with a delighted bow, when two shriveled little old women in tatters came chattering from nowhere, holding out their hands. "Who are they?" I asked Mr. Izak, while searching in my trouser pockets. "They are," said Mr. Izak, "aunts of the Oba." Maybe I had given my shillings to the last witnesses of the 1897 massacre!

On the road to Ife, Wahabi, motionless beside me, was doing his usual stunts at eighty miles an hour when suddenly a convoy of ministerial Chevrolets shot past us on a curve, while simultaneously a paranoid bus with the inscription "Prepare to meet Thy Lord," tried hard to squeeze through between the convoy and our Volkswagen. Exactly at this moment another question of the Oba shot back into my consciousness: "Tell me," he had said, sensing somehow that behind him on the bare wall I saw many ghosts, "tell me just in a few words, what exactly did you Americans do with the Indians who used to live all over your country?"

get him into focus and fell over one of his colleagues, tearing my trousers in the most strategic spot. Bleeding profusely, I found my camera mortally wounded under me. The sentry, standing not far away, for some reason or other presented arms and shouted, "Sorry!" as Africans will thoughtfully do when you stumble, choke on a fishbone, or have some other accident for which they are in no way responsible. The god smirked at me silently: "This will teach you, sonny. By the way, you didn't forget perchance to have your second tetanus shot, did you?"

The rest of the way to Ibadan, sitting full of anxiety on a burning patch of iodine, I prayed to the Great Spirit of Western Science to protect me.

Ibadan, city of hills, with interminable waves of corrugated iron roofs over ocher houses, is the largest purely African city in Nigeria. It has a population, mainly Yoruba in origin, of about half a million people. It seems to be all market, and at night twinkling with the tiny flames of millions of oil lamps, it lies against the hillsides as an enormous Christmas tree pullulating with life. By each small oil lamp the women in their blue dresses sit beside their little mound of merchandise, talking incessantly to neighbors and customers, the bronze of their faces beautifully highlighted in the unforgettable chiaroscuro. All night long this African outdoor life goes on, gregarious, gentle, and intense. From the pools of darkness comes deep-throated talk and the full-bodied laughter of men. The flicker of lamp-light discloses sudden glimpses of a baby at a full breast; through narrow deep alleyways tall women with hurricane lamps on their heads shuffle to nowhere and men in baggy pajama trousers and tentlike shirts saunter swinging chickens by their poor legs.

The huge new university, built in demonstrative modern style by British architects, is the pride of Ibadan, capital of the Western Region, and in its vast University College Hospital (recently built for a paltry seven and a half million dollars and looking more modern than any New York hospital) I received my antidote against the god of Ife.

Unfortunately there are no antidotes to protect one on the road from Ibadan to Lagos. It is a narrow racetrack of a road, full of traps and curves, along which every mile or so wrecks of brand new cars shout their *memento mori*. But they shout in vain. The human sacrifices of Ife and Benin may be over now, but the spirit of their carnivorous gods has triumphed. I saw the modern Yorubas with tense faces flying past in their cars at closest quarters, possessed by Shango, their old thunder god. Far from having been banished, and laughing raucously through the honking horns at the newly imported Saint Christopher medals and plastic Jesuses behind the windshields, the old god seemed

to leer at me. At every turn, wild with glee, he made feet press down on gas pedals or hands grab stupidly at emergency brakes.

I saw only a few of the sacrifices: the first was a single victim, her basket of chickens scattered over the road; then I saw the passengers of a mammy-wagon, with the inscription "Live and let live," strewn over the countryside close to a sign saying, "Happy Motoring." Shango may be cruel, but he has an African sense of humor!

Wahabi, possessed by his own god, the god of the tribe with the five tattoo marks on each cheek, steadily steered through the bedlam. Not far from Lagos, near a bridge, I stopped him in order to draw a small village with houses on stilts along a creek in suffused pink evening light. Dugouts with fishermen floated serenely by. A lithe young woman carrying fish strode majestically over a jungle path to the road.

Then the sky above Lagos became black and sheets of lightning seemed to beat down on the city. It started to pour. The car plowed through gulleys of water through deserted streets, blindly following the ghost of a taillight ahead. At the Mainland Hotel the doorman with his huge umbrella rescued me, and the cripples huddled together in a corner of the entrance shouted, "Evening, sah."

In 1960 the population of Nigeria was estimated to be about 38 million, with 18 million in the Northern Region and the remainder about equally divided between the Eastern and Western Regions. The Federal District of Lagos has some 325,000 inhabitaits. The largest city, and perhaps the largest truly African city of the whole continent, is Ibadan, with a population of 460,000.

The main racial groups are the Hausa of the North, the Yoruba of the West, and the Ibo of the East. The 3 million Fulanis in the North are non-Negroes of Mediterranean origin.

There are 250 distinct indigenous languages. The Hausa language is spoken by 40 per cent of the inhabitants. English is the official common language. The North is predominantly Moslem in religion; the West and East are partly Christian and animist.

Lagos, the federal capital, is Nigeria's most important port and handles more than 50 per cent of the overseas trade. The Niger and Benue rivers are traditionally the most important means of transport, but Nigeria has also railway lines and has increased its highway system by 50 per cent since World War II. This is reflected in the fact that the number of private cars has more than quadrupled since 1950.

Nigeria as an administrative unit was only created by the British in 1914, and, by the system known as "indirect rule," the traditional individuality of the separate territories was adapted to local government. The feudal and centralized traditions of the North made this system most effective there. As everywhere in Africa, pressures for self-government became

irresistible after World War II and the first spectacular postwar change took place in 1946, when elected members became a majority in the Legislative Council, which had jurisdiction over all of Nigeria. The Constitution of 1954 established a federal form of government. In 1957 a constitutional conference decided on self-government for the Eastern and Western Regions, and the Northern Region followed suit in 1959. On October 1, 1960, Nigeria became an independent member of the Commonwealth with a federal form of government, comprising the Western, Eastern, and Northern Regions, the District of Lagos, and the Southern Cameroons which later the same year voted for consolidation with the new state of Cameroun (formerly a French colony).

Nigeria is now a parliamentary democracy with a division of functions between the federal and regional governments. As in the rest of Africa, the political parties are mainly based on tribal and national differences: the Northern People's Congress is dominant in the North, the National Council of Nigeria and the Cameroons in the East, and the Action Group (which forms the parliamentary opposition) in the West. The NCNC is the oldest nationalist party and was organized in 1944 by Dr. Nnamdi Azikiwe. Dr. "Zik" and his party are convinced neutralists while the other two national parties favor a closer collaboration with the West.

Nigeria's economy has been expanding rapidly in the postwar period, but agriculture is still its main basis. The country is the world's largest exporter of palm products and peanuts. It also exports cocoa, cotton, rubber, and tin.

The country is nearly self-sufficient in food products. Cattle-raising is practical only in the North, because of the prevalence elsewhere of the tsétsé fly. Important mineral deposits of lead, zinc, and iron ore, as well as oil, have been only sketchily exploited. Nigeria is self-sufficient in coal production (chiefly near Enugu).

Educational facilities are showing rapid growth, although in the Northern Region nearly 90 per cent of the adults are illiterate as against some 50 per cent in the Western Region. The North is making progress in secular education, but is still lagging far behind. There is an abiding shortage of teachers in the whole country. The University College, at Ibadan; and the Nigerian College of Arts, Science and Technology, at Ibadan, Enugu, and Zaria, are the main institutions of higher education. University College confers University of London degrees and maintains the standards of that university.

6 / About a City and Animals

The seemingly never-ending flight from Lagos via Leopoldville to Nairobi crosses Africa from west to east over some of its most spectacular landscapes, over the gigantic volcanoes, forests, and savannahs of the Congo to Usumbura in Ruanda-Urundi, where Lake Albert, huge as an ocean, blinds you with its glare. Then the fertile plains of Uganda begin, and after gliding over the endless water desert of Lake Victoria, three times the size of Massachusetts, Entebbe is reached. It looks deceptively British, surrounded by Sussexlike hills dotted with cattle. In the airport restaurant in arid British waiting-room style, turbaned Africans silently serve tea with biscuits. It is only a short hop then to Nairobi, the capital of Kenya. The city is strikingly modern. It might be American-built but for that stuffy, arid *je ne sais quoi* which stamps things British by inventing signs like "Patrons are respectfully requested to refrain from expectorating while on the premises. Thank you," instead of, more directly, "No spitting."

Nairobi's mixed population mirrors that of the whole complex country. Of Kenya's six and a half million people, about 50,000 are Europeans, 150,000 Indians, and 5,800,000 Africans. Since the political power and the most fertile regions are entirely in the hands of the Europeans, while the economic power is monopolized by the Indians, it is not surprising that tensions were built up, which led finally to the Mau Mau uprisings.

Nairobi may look modern and relaxed, but its inner sullen tension will continue until a final solution to its politico-economic problem is found.

This city, financial capital of all East Africa, with its modern office buildings, hospitals, skyscrapers, and hotels, was built by British and Indians in a landscape which fifty years ago was still total wilderness. Realizing that the British also created the large plantations—although of course with the hands of native labor—one could hardly expect that all this would be simply handed over to the Africans at the first cry for independence. Will the British, despite the bloody intermezzo of Mau Mau in the early fifties and the bitterness which never disappeared, still succeed in slowly transferring their power in such a way that here, as in India and the Sudan, more Britishers will earn their living than ever before?

In the very English hotel I ran into Jim Harvey. After having been demobilized as an RAF pilot, like many others he found he could not say good-by to Africa and so he tried his luck as a big-game hunter with camera and rifle and became a safari organizer.

"You just have a few days here," he said, "why don't we get out of this infernal city? You don't understand it anyway. Nobody does. So let the people go to hell and let's go to the animals."

The Game Park is practically at the gates of Nairobi. At the entrance we were checked by a smartly uniformed African policeman, whose pierced earlobes stretched all the way to his shoulders like rubber loops. He pointed to a large sign warning visitors not to get out of their cars.

The high plateau of the park stretches endlessly to the horizon with its brown, parched grass and clumps of dwarfed trees under an immense opaline blue sky with wild feathery clouds. The Nairobi Game Park is an enormous reservation of forty square miles, where, only twenty minutes from the largest city in Kenya, thousands of wild animals live in complete freedom.

Flocks of strange birds flew up in front of our car, and out of the tall grass popped the ludicrously long necks of ostriches. Their contemptous eyes followed our movements with supercilious amusement. Dozens of herds of zebras were grazing peacefully, refusing to connect man with the gasoline vapors which envelop him here. Cars are to them strange creatures and relatively harmless, inspiring neither curiosity nor fear.

Under the trees, giraffes, nibbling the leaves of the higher branches, turned around once in a while to look at us with their large sentimental eyes, fluttering their long heavy eyelashes like over-made-up courtesans. Here and there wildebeests, or gnus, were grazing or ruminating quietly, their angry-looking, bison-like heads crowned by a disproportionate burden of horns. They stand high on their forelegs like giraffes, and seem to crouch on too short, gray hind legs decorated with black stripes as if they had rubbed them against freshly painted zebras. If the camel is really a horse put together by a committee, the wildebeest is a cow edited by an editorial board. They appeared alone or in herds. A group of six, their savage bovine heads raised, their manes flying in a gush of wind, seemed to be posing for an invisible academic sculptor.

Impalas, beige-brown, their fine thin heads pointing upward, their large ears quivering, their slender bodies beige and black striped on the flanks, flew past like a stroboscopic flash, without visibly touching earth. Large buck antelopes with magnificent horns and proud faces stared right into my eyes, transmitting clearly to me what it means to be an antelope. Here and there a small house emerged from the high grass, where an old Somali warrior was tending his herd of zebulike cows.

Close to a river, where crocodiles and hippos seemed to gather in order to see and to be seen, was a parking lot. A rustic path ran along the water. In the trees above our heads some fifty monkeys were chasing one another.

In the middle of the veldt a car was standing. Jim said, "It looks from here like a game warden's Land Rover." Slowly we drove closer until we saw a lioness, quietly suckling one cub while another cub crawled over her body like a kitten. Although our car was only five yards away, the lioness just lifted her head, gave an indifferent look, and relaxed again. Then she began to demonstrate her mother love by licking her cub like a well-behaved housecat. Time stood still as we watched her from the open car window. The lioness soon forgot the humans, her eyes closed, and she seemed to sleep with the cubs pressed against her body. But a little later, when one of them strayed too far in the high grass toward the car, her eyes opened. I heard no sound, but the cub returned to her.

A few hundred yards farther in the rough veldt, under a small tree, two lions were enjoying a siesta, as if they were lying in a hammock. They looked rotund and satisfied like big fat tomcats. They obviously had just lunched off zebra or gnu. The smaller one was lying on its back, his hind legs on a fallen tree, the way one puts his feet on a chair after eating too much. The larger one glanced at us, swished his tail, and looked the other

way. They both looked so tame and lazy that I was tempted to get out of the car and draw them at leisure. But I knew it was inadvisable. Recently an American couple tried to get friendly, as American couples will. The man got out of the car, his wife took a snapshot for the folks back home, in which her husband is seen smiling proudly. Then, to make sure, she took a second one. But on this one he does not smile. While the woman focused again, the lion turned around, quietly lifted its paw, and struck out as the shutter clicked. The man was dead of course.

Lions are so enormously strong—although in the vast veldt they look comparatively small—that one alone can carry off a gnu which would take ten men to drag away. They can accelerate within seconds from resting to a speed of 35 miles an hour. Later Jim showed me some of his collection of over 2,000 photographs. In one of the pictures a pair of lions are attacking a wildebeest. The animal is attacked from the back by the lioness, while the lion jumps to its throat. The poor wildebeest stands paralyzed in fear, a resigned expression in his eyes.

The peacefulness of the park is just as illusory as the apparent peacefulness of a big city suburb on Sunday.

"Are there no elephants here?" I asked Jim. "No," he said, "thank God. I had enough of elephants after my last elephant adventure; that happened in Kenya too," he continued. "My wife and I were driving our Land Rover cross-country, close to the Great Rift Valley, when far off we saw about half a dozen elephants approaching. I had already some respect for them, so

I stopped the car. They passed at a distance and my wife was very enthusiastic. This was the first time she had seen them in the savannah. But what followed was a real nightmare. All at once elephants seemed to be coming from everywhere, there were probably over a thousand milling around our car for more than eight hours, rubbing occasionally against the fenders and the hood which were completely ruined, and it was a sheer miracle that they did not upset the car or step on it. It seemed to last an eternity. My wife became hysterical and I kept my hand on her mouth, urging her not to move or make any sound. It seemed the only chance of survival. After eight hours they started to withdraw and I still don't know how we lasted that long. But not everybody was that lucky, for next day we were told that this same herd had kicked two cars over the escarpment of the Rift Valley into an abyss 1,500 feet below. Maybe the occupants in their mortal fear had started to yell or shoot or perhaps had blown their horns. Nobody will ever know."

Travel books on Africa abound in animal stories, and films on Africa still suggest a continent populated by big game and by natives who wear masks and dance all day and night. Only the newsreels show the Nkrumahs speaking at the UN in flawless English, the Tom Mboyas descending from jets in Chicago, and the crowds rioting in Leopoldville.

Actually, for the Western city dweller, there is nothing more unforgettable than the fleeting apparitions of the mysterious, teeming animal life of the continent, the sudden rustling in the underbrush, and the flash of a ringed coil retreating into the leaves; the few steps taken in the high grasses of a dry swamp to pick a papyrus stem, when in seconds ants have crawled up my trousers and overrun my body so that I pick them from my shirt collar; the scorpion staring at me from the folds of a

freshly ironed towel in a Khartoum hotel; the speedboat on the Ogowe River slashing a path through a compact cloud of mosquitoes; pelicans filling a majestic kapok tree like huge orange and white leaves; yellow-gold-and-black gendarme birds transforming a tall palm tree into a skeleton hung with hundreds of small global nests; a grove of trees at the roadside in the Congo suddenly changed into a circus with dozens of monkeys jumping and crawling from branch to branch, young ones clinging to their mother's bellies; baboons staring at me evilly from between the rocks of an Ethiopian mountain pass; the half-tame owl "Mexique" at Lambaréné, screeching for fish in the middle of the night and trying to land on my head; the glance into the eyes of the donkeys carrying impossible loads to the markets; the black face of a large ape peering through the crack of a wall of foliage on the Rivière des Pélicans; kingfishers diving from black silken sky into black velvet water and close by, too close by, seven pairs of small eyes and ears sticking out of the mirror-like river, all moving in unison with the movement of my boat, when a small herd of hippos feels intruded upon. . . .

In drawing them, sometimes only catching the flashing of a movement, I partook of all this animal life which lives on with me, and sometimes suddenly, in a hair-sharp vision, comes back as I turn the corner of a New York city block.

7 / Ethiopia: Island in the Sky

The DC-6 of Ethiopian Airlines was waiting on a brand-new runway of the Nairobi airport. The airport, just unveiled, looks so American that the Mau Mau seem to be farther away than Alaska. An Ethiopian DC-6 is not an ordinary plane. It is extravagantly decorated with red and yellow stripes and on its nose two huge red and yellow lions are painted. A sexy blond stewardess with a professional smile led me into an interior that immediately made an imperial impression. It was all done in gold and powder-blue leather on which innumerable imperial lions clambered toward the ceiling. Even the luggage rack was finished in gilded leather. The pilot looked familiar. He was the thick-necked man who last night, at the table next to me at the New Stanley Hotel in Nairobi, had been dining with the gorgeous stewardess in her strapless evening gown. I had immediately diagnosed him as a visiting Russian commissar, but he turned out to be a big Swede from Minnesota. Through the hoarse loudspeaker came his Midwestern American voice: "This is Captain Hansen welcoming you on flight number nine-one-seven to Addis Ababa. . . ."

From Nairobi to Addis is about three hours' flying time, but it might as well be three days. For we fly over an endless, timeless stretch of savannah, virgin forest, and desert, an enormous span of Nothingness without any sign of human life anywhere. Looking down, I realized that the story of Russians smuggling weapons to the Mau Mau overland from Ethiopia was ludicrous. There is no way of getting through.

Addis airport may be like airports all over the world; the city, however, does not remind you of anything ever seen. It is less Baedeker than the *Thousand and One Nights*. Addis has an altitude of about 8,000 feet, like Mexico City. But when you walk lightheadedly over Mexico City's boulevards you can dream that you are in Paris; in Addis Ababa you can only imagine that you are in Tibet. The city, with about 500,000 inhabitants, is haphazardly strewn over steep hills. On one of these hills is a small, disorderly but reasonably modern, shopping district and, miles away from it, on another hill, are the palaces of the Emperor, the House of Parliament—built to give an illusion of modern democracy—the embassies, and University College. This section looks international and elegant; there is even a modern apartment house, standing alone like a salesman's only sample, with an enormous abstract design on one of its walls. The Imperial Palace has gates like those of Buckingham Palace or the Elysée. But stray for a minute from this respectable avenue and you find yourself among huts of clay and straw with thatched roofs. Through streets, more often than not unpaved alleys of knee-deep mud, cows, chickens, and donkeys slosh contentedly. Tiny Fiats serve as a combination taxi and bus. They take four or five passengers whom they deliver where

Franck
Addis 59

...clergy, monks farmers and a gentleman

desired along the road for about a dime. I took one to the shopping district and my fellow passengers were Ethiopians in their long white togas. After some miles I found them a bit too fragrant and decided to walk the rest of the way. But this is a slow and painful exercise because of oxygen hunger at this altitude. I panted up a narrow street, where in every house men were making mattresses. In front of the dingy workshops full of mattresses loitered some of the women who ply their trade on them. From this back alley I turned into a real street.

Through the wide open doors of an official building, protected by sloppily uniformed sentries, I saw something that seemed to be an exhibition and I decided to have a look. Hundreds of large mounted photographs of His Imperial Majesty Haile Selassie I stared at me. They were all taken on Selassie's last trip in 1959: the Emperor shaking hands with Khrushchev, smiling at President Salazar, inspecting troops with King Baudouin, cutting a ribbon with Tito, and being dwarfed by de Gaulle. However, this small "big man" of Ethiopia cuts a fine figure in these

pictures. And well he may, because he is not only the Emperor, King of Kings, and Lion of Judah, but also his own foreman, school superintendent, FBI, and social reformer. With enormous energy and practically alone, he has tried within his lifetime of seventy-one years to pull Ethiopia from its deep medieval mud and to make a modern state of it. In the pictures he looks nobler than Salazar, more intelligent than Tito, wittier than Khrushchev, wiser than Baudouin, and at least as aristocratic as de Gaulle himself. But then, many Ethiopians I met looked as if their family trees, like the one of their emperor, might well extend back into the Biblical realm of King Solomon.

When I took a *gherrie* (a horse-drawn taxi) to the Ras Hotel, a mile downhill from the shopping district, I felt as though I were riding through a city populated entirely by kings and queens, even if they were wearing rags. If there is a country where people are more beautiful, I haven't seen it. The noblest features glow here in a deep golden ocher. People are poor and they cannot yet adorn their bodies with the fashionable junk of the twentieth century. Their dress is simple and of royal dignity. The men generally wear jodhpurs of more or less white material. Their upper garment is the so-called shamah, a roughly woven thin blanket, draped over both shoulders. White is the basic color with which all garments start, but time and weather do the rest of the coloring and produce shamahs in all shades of white, yellow ocher and sienna, to the deepest umber. Many carry a long staff as a cane, more a Biblical shepherd's staff than a walking stick. But this is a country of shepherds and warriors, and so the stick probably serves also as a weapon. I never met a peasant in the country without his staff—it is used to lean on, to climb with, or for beating the sheep and donkeys. Peasants, holding it in the back between their shoulders, walk around as if crucified.

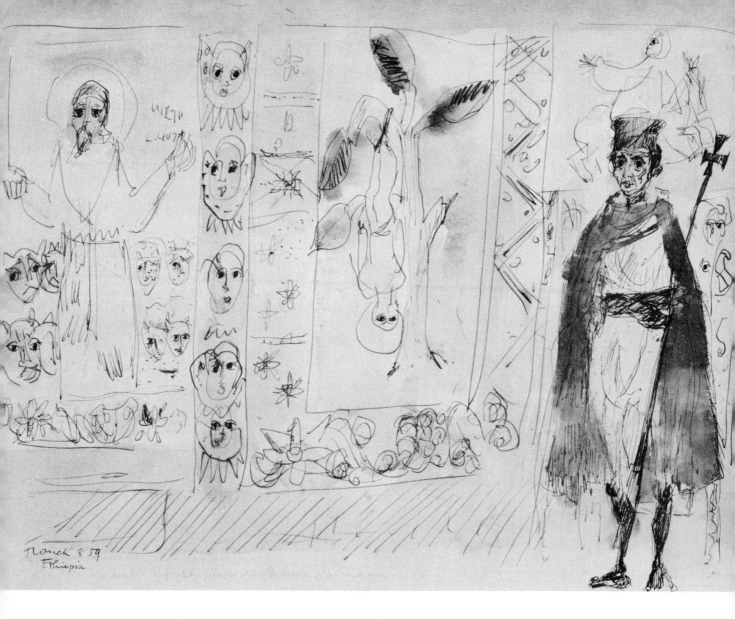

The women wear wispy white batiste dresses, embroidered with borders in sweetish colors. The long fairy-tale dresses fall down to the muddy bare feet or heavy black boots. Hair is built up intricately into crownlike structures, kept shining with butter, and covered by thin tulle veils of garish magenta or poisonous neon green through which the jet-black hair shines like dark jewelry.

Some people—were they workers or beggers?—wore cloaks sewn from innumerable pieces of rag and burlap, overlapping in shingles. Here and there pieces of leather were stuck on as in *collages*. Some of these cloaks looked like the half-burned Christmas trees found in the gutter after the holidays. Pathetic and magnificent, they clothed their owners in terribly human grandeur.

In the cold and the drizzle I sat down on the terrace of a small Italian café in order to draw these emaciated kings and queens. A young woman came begging at my table, she looked mentally disturbed. But her expression was tender and the skin of her smooth thin face had a deep golden ocher. Her dress was made of pieces of burlap from discarded potato or coal bags, with the half-effaced printing still visible through the grime. Her shawl too was made of this material. She did not actually beg, but stood still in front of me with an ecstatic expression, pressing a faded orange dahlia to her cheek. I gave her a coin and she bowed deeply like a medieval serf. Many Coptic priests passed by. They wore turbans and proudly carried their priests' staffs adorned with silver crosses, while they glanced at me out of the corners of their eyes. People bowed down to them and sometimes knelt as if for a foot kiss. The priest would interrupt the movement, catching the man under the chin with a mechanical but tender gesture, and give him on both cheeks the kiss of peace.

I saw old men in rags, noble-faced and with pointed beards, raise their hats or dirty pith helmets solemnly to each other, bowing like Victorian diplomats. There were hardly any fat people, except a few well-to-do bourgeois in their cars, Westernized, fleshly and commonplace. The general leanness is not only caused by poverty, but by the extraordinary number of fast days prescribed by the Coptic Church. Apart from the two set fast days a week, there are numerous other fasts, totaling some two hundred fast days a year, which, if strictly observed, makes dieting superfluous.

The Ras Hotel is like any other provincial hotel. The lobby badly needs painting, the red leather of the club chairs is torn and faded, the showcases are not filled with luxurious toiletries and jewels but with shoddy silver souvenirs, undelivered letters, dog-eared, used pocket books, and "lost and found" articles of all kinds. The architect who designed this hotel may not have been a Frank Lloyd Wright, but he had a strange sense of architectural humor. He put the dining room on the fourth floor but provided no elevator, and since there are no oxygen cylinders on the landings everybody enters gasping for breath. The reward for all this mountain climbing is rather disappointing: the view from the windows shows the biggest and best gasoline station in Addis, a few slummy streets, and on a distant hill a palace which, while looking like a boarding school, is reserved for visiting heads of state!

As I sat down, panting, at a table, a slender young man with the sensitive Ethiopian cast of features came to greet me. He was Yawand Wossen-Mangasha, Vice Governor of the Bank of Ethiopia. I had met him last year when, on his return trip from Harvard to Ethiopia, he dropped in at the Schweitzer Hospital in Lambaréné to pay his respects. We had liked each other immediately and renewed our acquaintance later in New York,

where he was a United Nations Delegate. Yawand Wossen is typical of the new generation of Ethiopian élite with the help of which the Emperor is modernizing his country in such a way that after 2,000 years of isolation it should become able to maintain itself in our complex, modern world. He was educated in London and Harvard and is now about thirty years old (I was relieved to learn that he survived the bloody abortive coup which shook Addis Ababa at the end of 1960). Actually all the highest officials here are between twenty-five and forty. Since the Italians carefully liquidated the whole Ethiopian intelligentsia during their occupation, it was necessary to start afresh after World War II. The Emperor is of Amharic race, and so is the noble family to which Yawand Wossen belongs. They are Africans of course, but Ethiopia, although part of Africa, does not look African. The majority of its people have no Negroid features and their complexion is more golden than brown or black. Psychologically too Ethiopia gives an impression totally different from the rest of Africa. One finds nowhere the

March 59
Addis

extroverted laughter and vitality of black Africa. The Ethiopian seems introverted, nearly melancholic. Although part of the population is Moslem or pagan, the Amharics were converted to Christianity in the fourth century. Their traditions date back to King Solomon.

About 1000 B.C., the Queen of Sheba visited King Solomon at Jerusalem. Who this Queen of Sheba was has never been precisely determined. The orthodox tradition assumes that she was the Queen of Axum in Ethiopia. Hungry for Solomonic wisdom, Her Majesty traveled to the Court in Jerusalem. Solomon, apparently frustrated by his 600 wives, felt irresistibly attracted to his beautiful dark visitor, but he promised to respect her person and not to touch her on condition that she would refrain from touching any of his property. Slyly however, the libidinous sage served his guest a very spicy farewell supper, and when in the middle of the night, plagued by thirst, the Queen drank from the royal water pitcher, Solomon claimed and received his compensation *in natura.* The Queen of Sheba left Jerusalem for Ethiopia pregnant with Solomon's child, later born at Axum as King Menelik I. The Queen sent the boy to Jerusalem, where he identified himself by the ring King Solomon had given to his mother, and he was educated at court. When he was about eighteen he returned to Ethiopia, accompanied by Hebrew nobles.

It is official dogma in Ethiopia that Menelik became the first ruler of the dynasty which continues to the present day, and every emperor of Ethiopia has claimed direct descent from the Solomonic line, hence the title "Lion of Judah."

After lunch Yawand Wossen took me to the Imperial Church near the Palace, where a Coptic service was being held. I felt I had been whisked back into the Middle Ages and had become

part of a Breughel painting. Mass was being celebrated. On the square in front of the church men and women—crippled, blind, and old, many of them beggars—were lying on the pavement in all possible attitudes. Before entering the church we had to take off our shoes. The nave was crowded with men and women in their white clothing, singing hymns with a terrifying intensity. The strange chant sounded obsessive, wild and prehistoric. We were conducted to the choir area in the middle of which a deep crypt gaped; around it stood the notables, leaning on their long silver-knobbed staffs and praying aloud. With a loud ringing of bells the curtains before the altar, where a priest in high gold miter and gold vestments was celebrating the Mass, suddenly closed. The whole congregation knelt, touching the floor with their foreheads. Behind the closed curtains the Mystery of Transsubstantiation was enacted. The curtains opened and Communion began. First came babes in arms, tendered to the priest by the acolytes, then small children, and finally the grownups. The priest offered the Sacred Bread, then acolytes gave each a spoonful of wine and passed a glass of water. The communicants covered their mouths with their *shamahs,* as if to protect the Holy Meal, and went back to their places. After Communion the priest raised a colossal silver cross and blessed the congregation. Then he descended from the altar and slowly walked through the whole church, stretching out his hands to the fervent kisses of the faithful.

Moved and speechless, we were swept by the crowd out of the church. Outside Yawand Wossen's Volkswagen was waiting (the Emperor does not like his dignitaries to have big cars!). We drove to the market, which in Addis is not a market at all, but a city in itself, a city for buying and selling. In the textile section tailors sit on the porches of the innumerable little shops and on all kinds of sewing machines make garments to order

from materials just bought inside. There are textile streets, shoe streets, hardware streets, hay streets, sheep streets, and antique streets. The hay streets are perhaps the most touching: a never-ending stream of small donkeys, buried under their burdens of hay, arrives from the surrounding countryside. These living haystacks with their patient and intelligent faces come from villages often forty miles away, led by patriarchs holding their long staffs. Eucalyptus branches too are brought to market from distant mountains by human pack animals—the women, who carry the enormous bundles on their backs, bent double, their silver crosses swinging between their tattooed breasts. Eucalyptus is used as fuel, baskets are made of its twigs, animals are fed with its leaves, and houses are built of its branches. All around Addis the eucalyptus spreads its silvery sheen over the landscape. Yet it was first introduced to Ethiopia by the Emperor Menelik II in the nineteenth century.

Is Addis really a city? It has its palaces, its enormous opera—which is not an opera, but a movie theater—its night clubs, ministries, brothels, and hospitals; its mud puddles, taxis, and gherries, its round Coptic churches, its mosques, its teeming market. So it must be a city. But in what city are people having their lunch on the tombstones of the largest cemetery? In what city is the mayor publicly flogged because something went wrong with the water supply? In what city do beggers look like kings, and where do the rich alight from their cars in order to prostrate themselves when far away the Emperor's coach is approaching?

From Addis Ababa I had to fly to Gondar in order to give my course at the Haile Selassie I Public Health College. Thanks to the Ethiopian Airlines it is just a three-hour trip. Ten years ago the 300 miles from Addis Ababa to Gondar took a week by road, except in the wet season when one could not reach it by car at all. And yet Gondar is one of the three or four largest cities of Ethiopia. This may give some notion of what a centralized government means in a country like Ethiopia! The airline was started in 1947 essentially as a branch of the TWA and the majority of the pilots are still Americans. But each year more Ethiopians are being trained and my pilot to Gondar was an Ethiopian. Since I survived, I have great respect for him! It is an unexplained miracle how Ethiopian Airlines has been able to fly these fourteen years without a single fatal accident through a country where there are no proper airfields, usually not even radio contact, not to mention the absence of control towers, radar, and similar refinements.

On the day of my flight there was only a freight plane available. It was an old C-47, a World War II veteran, affectionately known as the "Vomit-Comet," and outfitted with bucket seats arranged lengthwise. An Ethiopian steward belted the uninitiated to their seats. I sat close to the door on an ice-cold iron bench and as the door did not close tightly, I could study the frightening landscape through the gap: fertile meadows which ended suddenly in bottomless abysses, plains from which monolithic cliffs unexpectedly rose, so close that we seemed to touch them with our wing tips. At our first stop I looked out for the landing strip, but did not see anything that looked like one, until I noticed that we were coming down in a meadow, marked by two rows of whitewashed stones. The "Terminal Building" was a native hut on which a windsock was mounted. People wrapped in white blankets were standing motionless in the drizzle, carrying baskets of chickens and bundles of goatskins, which were thrown into the plane. The sumptuously dressed Moslem woman opposite me, who had snuggled against her skull-capped husband during the whole trip, stiff with fear, walked away from the plane proud and relieved, her pink-and-white dress dragging in the mud. The pilot was trying to tighten a loose bolt on one of the flaps. "Doesn't matter," he said to me, "I'll have it fixed when I get back."

We took off again, in a crescendo of vibration and noise, over the rocky, muddy ground. A drunken peasant, barefoot in his jodhpurs and shamah, had joined us. During the take-off he fell

on the floor. He lay there vomiting. The steward lifted him into his bucket seat and gave him a cardboard cup. The drunk lifted the cup to his eye and started to stare into it as if it were a telescope. He kept staring for an hour, absorbed in visions, and forgot about his vomiting. A man in a dirty pith helmet and raincoat, whose features had something Mongolian, was sitting next to him, motionless and utterly detached, as if there were no drunk, no plane, no noise for him. At the second stop the meadow was a mere puddle. A fountain of mud shot up which covered the windows. The plane seemed to be shaking to pieces. But it stopped intact, mud dripping from its flanks. "This is quite something," I said to the pilot. "What a field!" —"Oh, the next one, Debra Tabor, is much worse," he said. "That field has a hump you can't even see if there are cows grazing at the other end!" But we survived even Debra Tabor, although the plane skidded out of control for a few hundred yards and stopped with a fearful shudder. The pilot said, "Here I won't land on the return flight, I guess." The man with the pith helmet got off. Three small horses, with hanging heads, were waiting in the rain and a few dripping white figures stood silent at their side. When the man came out of the plane, they slowly started toward him and one after another knelt in the mud and kissed his feet. He had taken off his helmet and with a formal smile kissed each separately on both cheeks. They disappeared together into the fog, and the door banged closed once more.

Now my only fellow passengers were a man and his pregnant young wife, both barefoot and frozen with fear. They had the enormous dark eyes which stare at the spectator from Ethiopian church paintings. Eyes which do not seem to see, to observe, to measure, but visionary eyes passively encompassing a mysterious world. The woman was anxiously sucking a small lemon, her

Freuch '59
Ethiopia

safety belt tightened under the coming child. Her husband, a Byzantine John the Baptist, had their little girl in his lap. The child looked feverish. I gave her a piece of candy and the parents' eyes now focused on me with a ghost of a smile for the first time. All at once the couple became excited, forgetting their fear and pointing down to a miserable group of circular huts over which we passed. They had recognized their village!

And then came Gondar. The Director of the College, a round-faced American, Dr. Brooks Ryder, was waiting for me. In his Land Rover we bumped for miles through a Scottish landscape to the hospital with which the college is connected. This small white hospital of 150 beds, built by the Italians during the occupation, serves a whole province with a population of one and a half million people. Patients are often brought in, carried on a rough wooden stretcher by their families, who have walked over hills and valleys for a whole week: a clear and painful illustration of the medical need in Ethiopia, where a population of 20 million has to manage with some 120 doctors of whom about 80 live in Addis Ababa and Asmara. For the time being it is of course impossible to send a sufficient number of students to foreign medical schools to make up for this medical famine, although a disproportionate percentage of the national budget is spent on public health and education. That is why the Haile Selassie I Public Health College was founded in Gondar. Since the intention is to provide medical help for rural Ethiopia, it was felt that the school should be in the country instead of in Addis Ababa. Gondar was chosen because it was in the enviable possession of a hospital.

The college trains three categories of personnel: health officers, community nurses, and sanitarians. The health officers are given a four-year course in preventive medicine, mass treatment, and especially handling of epidemics. When they have graduated

they are not full-fledged doctors and can work only in govern-ment service. But for the work they have to do, they are better trained than any ordinary physician. Also I found that their knowledge of anatomy, physiology, and pathology was surpris-ingly good. They are not being trained in surgery: emergency cases still have to be sent from rural areas to base hospitals.

The community nurses, who are also trained as midwives, have a three-year course, and the sanitarians are technicians who get two years of training in subjects such as well-digging, insect control, and excrement disposal.

These three categories are trained together to form teams which can be sent out to set up rural treatment centers. Two years ago, during a terrible malaria epidemic which killed tens of thousands of people, these teams first proved their useful-ness. In the areas where health teams operated, thousands of lives were saved. Such an obvious success is enormously impor-tant in order to establish medical contact with the utterly ignorant population. Only spectacular demonstrations of success make it possible to gain acceptance of hygienic programs, which the people do not understand and hence suspect and sabotage.

An hour after my landing in Gondar I found myself standing in an amphitheater before a hundred students. I tried to feel my way, having no idea of what these young people could under-stand. I spoke about the prevention of dental disease, drawing big diagrams on a blackboard, and found that talking informally and telling a few jokes established a contact which I had never expected. During the first question period I was bombarded with intelligent questions, which showed that I could delve much more deeply into my subject matter. My main difficulty was that Ethiopian etiquette prohibits loud speech and all my questioners whispered their inquiries at me in their peculiar English.

The student nurses looked most charming, their black eyes full of interest, but they kept mum. It is against local good manners for women to speak up in male company. When I told them that in America it is about the other way around and that usually the woman does the talking, they were very much amused and slowly started to whisper questions too.

Next day my actual course for the Health Officers started. They showed such keen interest that my lectures, demonstrations, and clinics, which had been planned for three days, continued for more than a week. My demonstrations took place in the Operating Room, the domain of a German surgeon. He told me: "I lived in the East Zone and after surviving the Hitler mess without getting too involved, just doing my work in my hospital, I didn't feel like starting the same hide-and-seek all over again, so when the Communists wanted to draw me into their politics, I decided I had had enough and one night I fled in a rowboat to Sweden, and through a chain of coincidences I finally ended up in Gondar!"

What impressed me most in this college was that apart from an American director, a Chinese dean, and a German surgeon, there were also Danes, an Indian, a Pakistani, a Persian, Scottish nurses, and a Dutch bacteriologist working in perfect harmony. And even more impressive: the hospital and the college are financed and administered by four agencies, the World Health Organization, UNICEF, Point Four, and the Ethiopian Government. This small medical United Nations is proving every day that people, usually divided by national prejudices and even traditional antipathies, can work together fruitfully toward a concrete aim, not only without conflicts, but with a very special satisfaction in discovering that co-operation is possible.

On Sunday we drove to Kolla Duba, some fifty miles over a dirt road. It is the first rural health center to be used for the practical training of newly graduated health officers. These men had been unable to interrupt their urgent work in order to attend my course. So I started all over again for this small group in their clean, tiny clinic, built in the middle of the village with its round straw huts, in which the people and their animals live together. In this sea of mud a small group of enthusiastic young people are working on the improvement of health and the teaching of fundamental hygiene to their fellow Ethiopians. It is a heroic work.

From Kollu Duba the dirt road continues to Gorgora on the shore of Lake Tana, the enormous lake from which the Blue Nile springs. This river is of immense importance, since it fertilizes with its Ethiopian mud the plains of the Sudan and Egypt. Ethiopia could starve the Sudan and Egypt if it would deflect the waters of the Blue Nile. The Egyptians and the Sudanese are well aware of this decisive power in Ethiopian hands.

In Lake Tana float Coptic island monasteries, inhabited by monks so chaste that not only women, but all female animals are forbidden to land on their islands. This creates a problem for the monks. The donkeys and goats continually threaten to become extinct and if charity and piety do not supply new animals, the monks have them stolen on the mainland in order to replenish their flocks! There were ladies in our company, so we could not visit the monasteries, but fortunately we could visit a church, marvelously situated, overlooking the lake. According to custom, we took off our shoes and when we returned the shoes of one of the doctors had disappeared. The doctor ran around indignantly in his stocking feet, jumped in his car, and raced to the Police Station. After a short time the whole garrison of Gorgora appeared; some hundred and fifty officers and men began to comb the terrain around the church. This was a matter of Ethiopian honor! Rumors spread that the

thief had already been found, but in his deadly fear he had thrown the shoes away, these shoes which, to this poor Ethiopian, must have meant both capital and status. Suddenly there was a triumphal shout from the bushes on the shore: the shoes had been found, Ethiopian honor was safe, and the Army and the doctor stood there smiling sheepishly at each other, while clouds of mosquitoes, infuriated by the disturbance, attacked them. The thief was forgotten for the moment. Someone said that here, as in Saudi Arabia, his crime might still cost him a hand or a foot. Amputation was and, I was told, sometimes still is a punishment for theft.

We started back from Gorgora, racing over the bumpy road in order to get to Gondar before dark. In the dark the Castle of Gondar loomed gigantically above the low adobe houses.

The center of Gondar is the magnificent and grandiose Castle of Fasilidas, the Emperor, who between 1632 and 1667 smashed the power and influence of the Catholic missionaries. They were mostly Portuguese Jesuits, who had converted his father and become very powerful. The castle compound, built in Portuguese-Abyssinian style, is surrounded by high walls. The ruins of the twelve ceremonial gates are still standing, huge blocks of wine-red, moss-covered stone. Coptic churches, which are still

in use, were built within the compound, witnesses to the resurgence of the Coptic faith, encouraged by Fasilidas. Thus Gondar became the stronghold of tradition-bound Coptic power and remains so to this day. The castle was restored by the Italians during the occupation.

The Italians must have been possessed by a passion for building for most of the stone buildings—hospitals, movie houses, administration buildings, and so on—are of Italian origin. So was the small, comfortable government hotel where I lived.

For me the real center of Gondar was not the Castle but the much older, venerable tree in front of it. The tree has an enormous trunk which can be spanned by not less than six people.

In the tortured bark I could see images of all living forms: hands, bellies, breasts, heads, elephants' feet. Millions of insects live in the deep crevasses of its bark, innumerable birds nest in the gigantic umbrella of branches. This is the sacred tree, the tree of life and the tree of death. Under its canopy judgments were pronounced for centuries, and the guilty were hanged from its branches. Now herds of sheep and donkeys graze peacefully under the vast parasol of foliage and barbers shave heads on the grass underneath. When I sat down among them to draw, one of the most repulsive lepers I have ever seen sat down next to me to watch, and a man in rags, his legs as thick as pillars from elephantiasis, came begging. Soldiers in khaki, barefoot and dirty, their faces closed and suspicious, came to look at what I was drawing. In the wide streets buffalolike cows, emaciated horses, and small donkeys sloshed unhindered through the mud. Monks with their straw umbrellas begged resignedly in the drizzle. Turbaned priests in threes or fours, like patrols on mysterious errands, swished past in their long white robes and black cloaks.

At the end of the main street, which forms the backbone of Gondar and runs from the castle past many Coptic churches to the mosque, the market was humming. On the dirty pavement Moslem merchants were kneeling in worship. The skins of freshly killed sheep were drying on long sticks. Living sheep were carried on shoulders to the slaughter by white-gowned caricatures of the Good Shepherd. A fast had just ended and above the city hundreds of buzzards were circling. A nobleman on a mule, with his footman leading the animal by the reins, passed by. An antique bus full of people suddenly veered madly through the crowd, covering humans and animals with mud. In a dark little shop a silversmith was at work. Entering, I saw that the jewelry he produced was crude and commonplace, but in the dishes filled with old ornaments to be melted, I found beautiful things: Coptic crosses in endless variation, amulet cases, and a Star of David with a cross in the middle, symbol of Ethiopia.

I was lucky. The German surgeon offered to show me the Limo Loma Pass, one of the most spectacular mountain passes of Ethiopia. Next morning—a radiantly beautiful morning—we left Gondar and our Volkswagen started to climb the only road which leads from Gondar to Asmara, the capital of Eritrea. It is a strategic road built by the Italians. There are no crossroads, on both sides only impenetrable wilderness. In those mountains, valleys, and canyons, a few miles from the highway, even the police will not take the risk of exploring. But there are villages where the *shiftas* live. The shiftas are brigands, members and descendants of the Ethiopian underground during the Italian occupation, who never got used to the end of the war and have continued it on a small scale up till now. Actually they are a new edition of the traditional Ethiopian bandits. Every few months they stage an attack on a bus, or a truck is plundered and its driver killed. Our host himself, who once had the imprudence to use the road at night, was stopped, but the bandits left him unmolested when he proved that he was a doctor at the hospital, where they also go to be treated, if necessary—incognito of course. The shiftas are very hard to catch and I was told that some of the peaceful farmers along the road sometimes might well play shiftas at night.

As we climbed higher, clouds stormed at us from the valley until they enveloped the car completely. Here and there a few huts, huddled together, would emerge from the fog. Then visibility became absolutely nil and, driving slowly, we got stuck in herds of sheep and cows who would stampede in panic to all sides. The road continued through muddy villages, barely visible in the swirling clouds. Men on small horses, their rifles slung over their shoulders, emerged, white on white, like ghosts in a ghostly landscape. The horses, not used to cars, reared and galloped off into the fields. Heavily laden donkeys and mules

wisely plodded out of our way, but the panicky drivers confused them by their blows, and the animals trudged back to the middle of the road, blocking us. Half-naked children sat by the roadside looking after their cattle. They had their straw raincoats—small woven portable tents—pulled over their heads like large Manila envelopes.

Suddenly a man on a white horse loomed up, right in front of the car. The horse reared wildly and tried to jump onto the high embankment, but its rider pulled it backward and in a flash of horror we saw the horse fall on its back, on top of the man. For a long moment everybody seemed petrified. When I could move again, and leaped out of the car, hopeless because I thought it was all over, the man crawled out from under the horse, which was lying with all four legs stretched upward. The rider straightened his shamah, picked up his umbrella and rifle, grinned, and began pulling the horse's reins. Horses give up easily and after an accident they seem to assume that they are dead. The animal started to stir now with bewildered, stiff movements. "So I made a mistake," the motions seemed to say, "I am not dead yet!" Slowly the horse got up. Without a word the man swung himself into the saddle and still silent rode away.

There were no cars on the road all day long, only one truck and one bus came creeping up a sharp hill toward us, keeping each other company. Here and there along the road stood the remains of big walled farms, built by the Italians, but destroyed or ruined by neglect after the war by the Ethiopians, who could have used them so well.

The road rose higher and higher until after a few hours it seemed suddenly to drop into an abyss. This was the top of the Limo Loma Pass, a road hewn out of the sheer cliff with incredible imagination and persistence by the Italians in those few years of their occupation. They had even found time to build

March. 8.59

a monument here and there or a belvedere. On the monuments were the names of scores of men who had died during the construction of the road; to be more precise, the names of the Italians: the countless Ethiopian victims were not mentioned.

Now and then the clouds parted. Eagles swooped down a few yards away into the abysmal wild landscape of towering rocks and steep canyons, spread out as far as the eye could reach. Gotthard, Simplon, and Furka passes are child's play compared to the Lima Loma. In some of the hairpin curves I could think of nothing better than closing my eyes, while hanging on to the doorhandle of the car. Once down in the plain we had to climb up again for the return trip, alas. This seemed utterly impossible, although we had just descended: all that was visible was a sheer rocky cliff, miles high.

I had heard that on the high plateau there were some Falasha villages and I wanted very much to visit one. Falashas are Ethiopians, who, as far as one knows, have lived like the other Ethiopians in this country from time immemorial and who ethnically do not differ from them. Yet, they speak their own dialect and are not Christians but Jews, although their Judaism has heavy admixtures of the pagan and Christian rituals of the country. There was a time when they were the mightiest warriors of Ethiopia and their dynasty the dominant one. After they were defeated in the sixteenth century, they withdrew to their villages around Lake Tana and to the high plateau around Gondar. According to their own tradition they descend from the Israelite nobility which accompanied the first Ethiopian ruler Menelik on his return from visiting his father Solomon in Jerusalem. But it is more likely that these Ethiopians were some fifteen hundred years ago converted to Judaism by Jews from Egypt and Yemen. At any rate, they still feel exiled from the Promised Land and have not lost their Messianic dream. Until a few years ago they lived completely isolated, having as little social intercourse as possible with the surrounding population, worshiping in their synagogues, led by their own priests or even monks. Originally the Falasha monks consecrated the priests, but things are changing and, apart from two graybeards who are still alive, the monks have died out and the priests now consecrate each other. For a while a mission from Israel tried to rejuvenate the rapidly degenerating religious life of these Ethiopian Jews. There was even a move afoot to interest them in immigration to Israel. The Falashas were enthusiastic, but Israel's plans about the Falashas' role in the Jewish community seemed ambiguous and indecisive and the Falashas now have lost all hope.

I had heard that until recently Falashas could not own land, although they leased it, that they lived from some cattle-breeding and from plying the trades which in Ethiopia carry a stigma: they are weavers, blacksmiths, and especially potters. According to the superstition, which is still very much alive, potters and blacksmiths especially have the evil eye. Also, they can transform themselves into hyenas at night and kill cattle. In many primitive cultures the blacksmith, who works with fire and minerals, is a kind of magic figure because of his ties with the telluric world. The Amharic people, however, look down not only on blacksmiths and potters but on all menial labor; they are a people of shepherds, peasants, warriors, and priests. This arrogant contempt for the creative hand of the artisan may well be one of the factors which has retarded the development of Ethiopia.

We could drive quite close to the village Wolleka, but then we had to walk a muddy path leading from the highway to the first huts. It was a strange community. The village is built on the hillside on two levels and from the higher one other Falasha settlements in the valley are visible. Each village consists of a handful of *tukuls,* round straw huts of various sizes with pointed roofs. The families living there are always related. Like the other Ethiopians they wore shamahs made of hand-loomed, rough, unbleached material. It was surprising to see in a Jewish village women's dresses embroidered with a cross design. On the top level of Wolleka I met its patriarch Golla Tessema, with his wife, Asselefech Elias, surrounded by their children and many grandchildren.

I said I wanted to buy some of their pots. Immediately I realized that I was not dealing with primitives and that these people seemed to be gayer and milder than the rural Amharics I had met. The grandmother, Asselefech, had an extremely intelligent expression. A great sense of humor showed in the black eyes under the white bobbed hair. With the dignity of a great lady she led us into her primitive tukul with its clay floor, where chickens were gaily cackling around between two enormous barrels made from superimposed clay rings and serving as grain silos.

"I look dirty, because I am at work now," she said casually, "but I have also cleaner clothes," and she proved it by producing from behind the grain barrels the immaculate white dress which I later bought from her. She also excused herself, like any good housewife in Marseilles or Indianapolis, because her house was not quite in order; she had not expected guests. She offered to make coffee in one of the long-necked earthenware crocks which were baked in her own kiln, and started at once to pound the coffee beans in a mortar with a pestle.

Her husband was more reserved and went on sewing a shamah in front of the hut, surrounded by his grandchildren, as if I did

March 8 '59
Ethiopia

Fraull 8.59
Frbada.

not exist. I tried out the few words of Hebrew I know, and the woman looked at me with delight and ran outside to get her husband. He then immediately started searching behind the grain barrels and produced a calendar with Hebrew text which he showed me radiantly, but which neither of us could read. Then Asselefech Elias dived behind the barrels to find a cheap plastic wallet and showed me with pride photographs of a son, who is a teacher in Gondar, and of another son, who even is a clerk in one of the ministries in faraway Addis Ababa.

We had become friends and I could start to draw. "Don't make me so old," said the patriarch looking at my sketchbook and shaking his enormous, Biblical head with the twinkling not-at-all-evil eyes, "I'm only sixty-eight years old." His wife started to collect the clean pots for me to choose from and I went outside. A few steps away was a tiny tukul, just big enough for one man to sit in, and here one of the sons-in-law was weaving. The small hut enclosed him like a tea cozy. The primitive loom was on the mud floor, the weaver sat on the ground and his legs, which moved the pedals, were hanging down in a hole in the earth. His young and very handsome wife was standing next to the hut. She smiled and giggled coquettishly. The baby on her back was, as everywhere in Ethiopia, carefully covered with a shawl, because the sun is held to be extremely dangerous for children. After a while the mother also covered her face with the end of the shawl in mock shyness, but her large black eyes kept flirting with me.

Children with dolls in their arms came to look at my drawings. The dolls, of baked clay, were more than just toys and resembled Cycladic statuettes, prehistoric Greek fertility symbols, which here seem to have survived for innumerable centuries. I bought five or six of them and they are a greater treasure for me than the beautiful pots baked by Asselefech. She admired my drawing. "I can't draw," she said, "but I can make faces of clay and bake them." From under a pile of clothing she pulled a bas-relief portrait of her husband, which she had baked in clay.

The skills of the Falashas are doomed to disappear. In the market they now have to compete with cheap mass-produced crockery from Japan and aluminum pots from Germany. The blacksmiths have to compete with imported machine-made plow shears and implements. Moreover, the easily accessible iron ore deposits are becoming exhausted. Machine-made fabrics are also taking the place of hand-woven cloth.

Later I met a missionary of the Seventh-Day Adventists, who conduct a mission school in the Falasha country. He was proud that some Falasha children, eager as all Africans for education, had run away from home in order to attend his school, which gave him the opportunity of making Christians out of them. "Unfortunately," he said, "I can't make Seventh-Day Adventists out of them, because the government won't allow it. By the time we have them ready to be baptized, we have to give them to the Coptic Church, for, alas, they have the monopoly of baptism." "Do you find the Falashas very different from the other Ethiopians?" I asked him. "Oh, that is hard to say," he said, "they are of course much cleaner because of their endless ritual bathing (the surrounding people say that they can 'smell' a Falasha, because he smells of water!). They are also more honest, they don't steal so much. Maybe they are a little healthier, too, because of their dietary laws. But within a short time now, they'll certainly be absorbed into the general population. Isn't it a pity we can't make Adventists out of them?"

Ethiopia's population is estimated to range from 12 to 22 million. The federated state, 400,000 square miles in area, consists of Ethiopia proper and Eritrea. Its extreme variety of altitude (from 300 feet below sea level to over 15,000 feet above) is responsible for great contrasts in climate.

The country, governed by Emperor Haile Selassie I, is a constitutional monarchy with a bicameral parliament. The population is multiracial, the Amharas being the politically dominant group, the Hamitic Gallas (about 40 per cent), the most numerous.

Some seventy different languages are spoken. The official language is Amharic, which after Arabic is the most widely spoken Semitic language.

The Amharas, the ruling ethnic group, are of Hamito-Semitic origin and have Caucasian, not Negroid, features. Their color is golden ocher rather than black (the word "Ethiopian" to the Greek ear meant "sunburnt face"). There are, however, Negroid tribes in the South and the West.

In religion the Ethiopians are 57 per cent Coptic and 20 per cent Moslem, with 23 per cent divided among other religions, including pagan. The Coptic Church dates back to the fifth century and is one of the oldest Christian churches. The word "Copt" is derived from the Arabic *kibt,* which in turn is derived from the Greek *aigyptios,* or "Egypt." Saint Anthony (c. 270 A.D.) is one of the oldest Christian saints, one of the desert monks who have flourished in the Egyptian Church ever since. In the fifth century the Coptic Church separated from the Eastern Church on the issue of Monophysitism, the doctrine which denies the dual nature of Christ. Apart from adherence to this doctrine, Coptic religious practices resemble Greek-Orthodox more than Roman Catholic. The Coptic religion is strongly interwoven with national creeds and superstitions. Islamic influences are responsible for the rites of circumcision and the dietary laws.

It is estimated that one of every seven male Ethiopians is a priest, whose general education is on the whole very primitive. The influence of the Coptic Church on contemporary Ethiopian politics is still considerable.

Economically Ethiopia is an agricultural country with great potentialities. Exports are mainly coffee, hides, cereals, grains, wax, and spices. There is budding industry, mostly foreign-owned: cement, salt, sugar-processing, and cotton goods. Handicrafts are stunted in their development by the complex traditional taboos.

The country is probably 97 per cent illiterate, but under the rule of Haile Selassie I (since November, 1930) education is expanding. Addis Ababa, the capital has a university college.

8 / Stopover in Khartoum

In three hours you can fly from Ethiopia to Africa. Is not Ethiopia in Africa then? Yes, it is, but it is not of Africa. It is like an island in the African sky, an island peopled by insular tribes of silent mountaineers.

Over the airport of Addis hangs a foggy ice-cold drizzle. Three hours later, after following the Blue Nile, a thin, winding endless snake, the plane loses height and the thin snake becomes a wide river in the shimmering yellow haze. When the doors of the plane are opened in Khartoum, it feels as though a wet hot towel is slapped at you.

Mr. Kabbabe, a young light-skinned Syrian, who with his five brothers heads an import firm established in the Sudan for three generations, was there to meet me. He spoke American English, and could as well have driven from Brooklyn to pick me up at Idlewild. A fat, fatherly immigration officer, a holdover of the British administration, asked for my passport. He was the first African immigration officer I had seen who seemed unaffected by contagious megalomania and to whom the stamp he put in my passport did not appear to mean a symbol of personal power.

Khartoum is a widespread town of yellow dust and low white houses. Except for the noon hours, when people sleep in their rooms, on their roofs, under trees, in the squares, in all possible attitudes of shameless abandon, Khartoum is exuberant with feverish life, lived outside in continuous gregariousness and an

127

endless twitter of conversation. The coffee houses, counting by the hundreds, are brimming over with people until deep in the night. Black faces are constantly moving in laughter, talk, and quarrel, black hands fluttering out of the sleeves of the white nightshirtlike gowns with violent compulsive gestures.

There seems to be only one hotel worthy of the name, the Grand Hotel overlooking the Blue Nile, which half a mile upstream meets with the White Nile near the Omdurman Bridge. The two streams, refusing to mix their waters, continue together toward the plains of Egypt. The Grand Hotel is the social center of Khartoum. Khartoum (the name means "elephant's trunk") consists actually of three cities. The predominantly European city of Khartoum itself was founded by the English and laid out in star pattern like the Union Jack, not only out of exaggerated English patriotism but for sound strategic reasons. In this way the streets could be dominated from the center with a limited number of machine guns! Then there is North Khartoum, which is mainly industrial, and finally Omdurman

across the Nile, the original city and largest of the three. Omdurman, where 140,000 Sudanese live—but no foreigners—is the classical African native city with a famous camel market. The total population of the three "cities" is 250,000, including some 5,000 whites.

The Grand Hotel, down-at-the-heels and old-fashioned but still grand in its way, must have been symbolical of imperial Britain in its heyday. The terrace on the Nile and the bare dining room still hide some ghosts. Late at night, when the vulgar crowd of German industrialists, American oilmen, greasy Levantine traders, and Dutch engineers had left with their high-heeled, painted ladies, I could see the ghosts: British officers with clipped mustaches, spotless uniforms, and swagger sticks chatting quietly with the élite of civil servants from the Sudan Political Service—once described as "the most efficient and incorruptible colonial service the world had ever known. Its members had not been selected for their intelligence or brilliance, but for their sense of duty, their physical prowess and even their size." But now they are ghosts; among them sat their thin bloodless wives, discreetly showing their buck teeth in conventional smiles. At neighboring tables sat other shadows: round-faced British businessmen and commercial travelers noisily telling jokes in Midland accents. The two ghostly groups were self-contained, ignoring each other completely.

The old fat Sudanese waiter, his red cummerbund drawn tight over his belly, seemed to listen to the ghosts' conversation, too, and stared motionless over the dark, swift-flowing water of the Nile below. Then he saw that I was drawing in the bad light of the electric bulbs and was puzzled. To find out what I was doing, he came over and warned me of the large black insects crawling on the terrace and over my shoes. "They sting and you swell up like a balloon," he said.

Next day I had to lecture at the Kitchener Medical School. On the terrace, with the Nile shimmering in the blinding sun I could not even read my notes. The heat melted my brains and welded my thoughts into an amorphous mass. I tried my room, which was huge and Victorian and the four-foot fan lazily swished around above the mahogany bed. For hours I struggled with my own lecture notes, just lying on the damp hot sheets; later in the questionable tile bathtub, filled with tepid filtered Nile water, I lay staring at the heavy brass fixtures.

An hour before the lecture I got out of the tub and apathetically dressed in jacket and bow tie. But when I faced my audience, a whole amphitheater full of African medical students, boys in open shirts and girls in native dresses, my opening words were: "Ladies and gentlemen, since I am the only person here in a jacket and tie, I'll start my lecture by taking them off."

My partial striptease relaxed my audience, but I lectured with the sweat dripping into my eyes, so that I saw them as if through tears.

As everywhere in Africa, the audience was much more interested and concentrated than I had expected and the many questions asked showed how well the students had listened. The Kitchener Medical School, and nearly all the other institutions of learning in the Sudan, are British creations. When the country became independent in 1956, there were eleven teacher-training colleges in addition to the University of Khartoum, originally the Gordon Memorial College, founded in 1902. The university has faculties of arts, science, agriculture, engineering, law, veterinary science, and medicine, and has over a thousand students. When Kitchener in 1898 entered Khartoum and completed the reconquest of the Sudan, there were two schools in the country teaching secular subjects. The number of schools is now about two thousand! Thus the English have gaily dug their own grave all over the world by educating the people who, after having been educated, immediately started preparations to get rid of British rule. Now that the British are no longer the masters, they are generally respected and liked more than other whites. Syrians and other Levantine people, having been naturalized

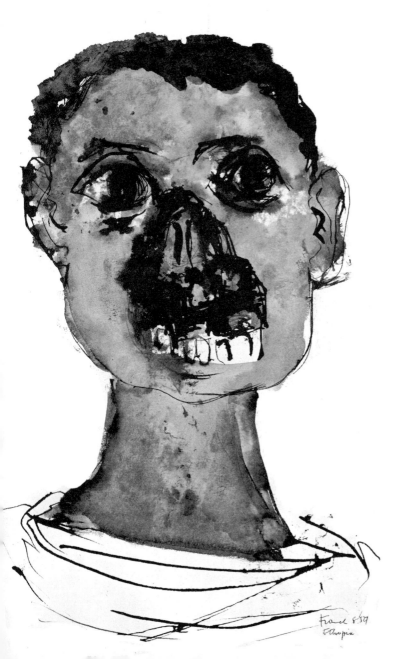

Sudanese for generations, now feel insecure and threatened because their light skin gives them away as not being "really" Sudanese. They speak nostalgically of British rule, for under the British all Sudanese were treated alike and impartially. Now, a young Sudanese official referred to my Syrian friends as "foreigners" who were there on sufferance. As everywhere in Africa, the best recommendation is a black complexion. I say black, because the golden color of the Indian is not dark enough. Still, in every country I found Europeans who wish to serve Africa simply because they love it and want to be part of its awakening.

One of those was Dr. Taylor, Professor of Surgery at the Kitchener Medical School, who, retiring after a brilliant career in London, decided to devote the remaining years of his life to teaching surgery in Khartoum. "Come and have dinner with me tomorrow," he said. "Whatever you may think of my cuisine, it will at least save you from getting dysentery at the Grand Hotel." The old man lived alone with his servant in a small villa. The dinner was simple, the cooking good, his wine excellent. The vitality and culture of the old professor, overcoming the unbearable climate of Khartoum, were exquisite and on his table were the most thoughtful books of the decade. "It is a bit hot, this country," he said, "but here at any rate there is no retirement age and I feel I am still useful. Very useful indeed!"

Next day he showed me cases at his hospital: sick children with wasted limbs, hideous swollen bellies of *kwashiorkor* (a deficiency disease), children with infantile paralysis in respirators, children between life and death, jaws eaten away by the gangrene of cancrum oris. Here and there a mother in a long, royal-blue dress, her face completely covered with an orange cloth with slits for the eyes, was sitting beside a bed, talking to her dying child.

He led me through this whole inferno of suffering seen in every hospital all over the world, this terrible and useless demonstration of a fragility and mortality that all living beings have in common and from which we refuse to learn that all our racial and national differences, our hatreds, recriminations, and discriminations are but sinister jokes.

I stepped out of the hospital and waved the taxis away. I wanted to walk. The great Mosque of Khartoum was trembling in the heat and the fierce sun. Its pink stone looked like colored sugar that might melt away in seconds. Wherever there was a patch of shade people lay stretched out, their faces against the earth. A fine swirling dust cut into my skin and my neck was rubbed raw by my shirt collar. My nose and throat seemed to be full of hot, melting sandpaper.

In the dark cave of a café two taxi drivers gestured at me. "Omdurman," I said. The Nile bridge seemed to shake and shiver in the noon heat as if it would explode, but nothing happened. We turned into Omdurman, the native city, dominated by the tomb of the Mahdi in the middle of a huge yellow square, made of dust and tears. The tomb made no sense to me architecturally; it is as monstrous as the Moslem fanaticism for which it stands.

This long-looked-for Mahdi, the "Guide of Islam," was Mohammed Ahmed, a Dongolese, who in a few years gathered an enormous following among the superstitious inhabitants of Kordofan. He was regarded by his adherents as the true commander of the faithful, who, filled with divine power, was destined to conquer the world. His fanatical followers became dervishes (begging friars) in their characteristic uniform, the jibbah. The Mahdi preached universal equality and community of goods and denounced all other Moslems in the belief that he was sent to wreak Allah's judgment on them. In 1885 his almost invincible army swept over the Sudan, capturing Khartoum and killing General Gordon.

The Mahdi died soon afterward and was succeeded by his even more extreme lieutenant, the Khalifa Abdullah. The Khalifa had long been the Mahdi's chief supporter and under his rule of cruelty, deceit, and mismanagement, the agricultural and economic ruin of the Sudan was completed.

The Mahdi's tomb in Omdurman became a place of pilgrimage which even substituted for a pilgrimage to Mecca.

The Khalifa's house, now a museum, is directly beside the tomb on the enormous square, where the stench of sweat and blood has long been burned away by the Sudanese sun. Inside the cool house the flags of the fanatics, torn and bloodstained, still made me shiver. In glass cases were old yellow photographs, a moving last letter from Gordon, and the heavy iron chains with which the priests and nuns, prisoners in the Kha-

lifa's dungeons for years, were welded to the walls. His European captives were flogged and badly mistreated but never killed.

In 1898 Kitchener reconquered Khartoum and the infamous Khalifa was killed in battle in Kordofan in 1899.

The camel market was nearly deserted. A few camels were lying on their sides like corpses, and vultures waddled distractedly between heaps of manure. In the shade of a mud wall some men were sleeping. The bazaars whirled with people; over blazing blue and white gowns, orange skullcaps and huge turbans crowned aquiline, Hamitic, and round Negroid faces. Through the thick hot air came a deafening din of shouting men and haggling women, braying donkeys and bleating goats. Cars honked slowly through congested narrow alleys, pushing loose-legged Sudanese on donkeys before them. On their mats on pavements and roofs, men turned toward the East in prayer, mechanically bending down and rising up. In dark holes-in-the-walls bearded men were hammering silver and brass and embroidering white cloth with white thread.

I arrived at the new suburban house of Mr. Kabbabe on the outskirts of Khartoum. There was some uproar inside: Mr. Kabbabe had just succeeded in killing a tarantula with a soupspoon!

The Republic of the Sudan is a vast plain (900,000 square miles, depending on the Nile River for irrigation. The Nile is formed near Khartoum by the confluence of the Blue Nile and the White Nile. Of the 11 million population, 10 per cent is urban. The political and economic capital is Khartoum with 110,000 inhabitants. Omdurman, its twin city, has 140,000. The seaport is Port Sudan. Forty per cent of the population is Arab, and the other 60 per cent is made up of Nilotics or Negroid Beja, Western tribesmen, Ethiopians, Egyptians, and Lebanese Syrians. Trade and industry are monopolized by the Europeans, Egyptians and

Syrians. The official language is Arab and only in the South are African languages spoken.

The official religion is Islam. Religious brotherhoods among the Moslems are important political and communal factors. In the South, African religions prevail, but there has been some conversion. For many centuries the South has been the victim of continuous slave-raiding by the Arabs.

For most of its 4,000 years of history the Sudan has been subjugated to Egypt, Rome, Byzantium, Turkey, Britain, and the Moslem empires. In 1898 Kitchener re-established British rule, which resulted in the modern organization of the Sudan government, the abolishment of slave trade, and the beginning of modern education. Although the vast majority of the population is still illiterate and education is not compulsory, the government is providing primary education in both urban and rural areas. The government also maintains teacher-training schools and technical schools, and recently the missionary schools in the South were integrated into the government school system. Khartoum University was established in 1956 as an integration of the Gordon Memorial College and the Kitchener School of Medicine. There is also a technical institute.

During the British "condominium" government the general improvement of public health was spectacular. Scourges like yellow fever, smallpox, cholera, sleeping sickness, yaws, and leprosy were brought under control.

Ninety per cent of the population derives its living from agriculture, with cotton as the most important export. The Gezirah Scheme between the Blue and White Niles is the most important provider of the nation's cotton, which accounts for half the national income. Thirty thousand farmers manage the scheme jointly with the Gezirah Board. Industry is embryonic.

On January 1, 1956, the Republic of the Sudan was founded as a parliamentary democracy, but in 1958 this was replaced by the military dictatorship of Ibrahim Abboud, Commander in Chief of the Army, and all political parties were dissolved.

The underdeveloped Negroid South constitutes a dangerous problem. It is anti-Arab, not only because of differences in language, customs, and level of civilization, but also because of the recent memories of slave-raiding from the North.

9 / The Congo:
Threshold of Chaos

When I first entered the Belgian Congo in 1958, the Belgians had not yet committed their "generous and spontaneous act" of giving the country independence. In fact, it would have sounded preposterously subversive to have predicted at a party in self-confident Leopoldville that this "model colony" might be independent even ten years hence. Had not a British colonial secretary, Lord Chandos, recently wondered in public whether the Belgians had not perchance hit on the only successful colonial policy?

True, since Stanley in 1874—"a determined, ugly little man with a strong American twang," as Queen Victoria had described him—had met with Livingstone in the wilds of the Congo basin, Belgian policy had not always been admirable. But even before the formation of the infamous Congo Free State at the Berlin Conference (1884–85) the unhappy land had been far from a paradise. It was perhaps the African country most ravaged by the slave trade, which at its height saw 50,000 men, women, and children yearly dragged to the Americas, not counting those kidnaped from their villages by the Arab slave traders. It may well be that the Congo lost a total of thirty million people, more than twice the present population.

From 1886 until 1908, the year before Leopold II died, the Congo was the personal property of this fun-loving monarch, a personal property seventy-seven times the size of his European kingdom. Atrocities, forced labor, and indignities were the order of the day. A scandalized European opinion, not yet used to a daily diet of mass atrocities, forced the Belgian state to take over Leopold's legacy. However, the Congo was not to be controlled henceforth by the Belgian Parliament but by a trinity of big business, the Church, and the Belgian Government. The Governor General was responsible only to the Belgian crown. Neither the white settlers nor the Congolese had any real voice in government until 1957, when a semblance of local government was initiated and general elections were introduced for the first time.

Yet all seemed rosy enough on that warm day in 1958 when I stepped off the plane at Leopoldville's brand-new glamorous airport. Leopoldville exuded prosperity; I did not yet know that its African population had doubled in the last few years and that most of the newcomers from the rural areas had no work and lived on the pockets of their relatives and not only on their pockets, but, because of inevitable housing shortage, on their premises as well. The "Belge," the native quarter of which you catch glimpses along the excellent road from the airport, was dangerously overcrowded with demoralized young people who had come in search of pleasure and riches but had found neither. Criminality had risen sharply and although the man from INFORCONGO, the official information service, called the "Belge" safe, even at night, no white inhabitant of Leo would accompany me there on foot, and if I went by car I was told I would be well advised to be extremely careful: "In case of an accident, even the most innocent one, just step on it, if you value your life!"

Meanwhile, on the main boulevards a mile away, the Belgians sat on their café terraces shouting, "Boy!" and ordering beers, waving to their friends in the unending parade of expensive cars on the wide avenue. In front of snooty shops, filled with the latest Brussels novelties, Belgian wives parked white convertibles. In tearooms, famous for their incomparable Belgian pastries, Flemish matrons were adding more pounds to their Rubenesque hips. Those pastry shops had also little windows for "outgoing orders," but these were reserved for the use of Congolese who wanted to buy sweets and of course were not allowed inside. At the bank, where I had to change some traveler's checks, a dozen or so Congolese queuing up in front of the teller's window hastened to make way for me; one, who was still counting his money, was being hurried by the black cashier behind the window in order to let me pass. At the post office the same comedy was played. I felt strangely humiliated by these people who stepped aside automatically without expression in their eyes—I was not a man to them; they were reacting mechanically to the White Man.

The Hotel Memlinc is luxurious and ultra-modern. A cool, illuminated fountain twinkled in the spacious lobby and young Africans in trim pale-blue uniforms were at one's beck and call. Some of them smiled constantly and all shouted, *"Oui, monsieur!"* to everything you said. It took me some time to realize that they hardly knew French. To get a cup of coffee and a roll, you had to fill out a slip. The telephone numbers you asked for (*"Oui, monsieur!"*) were invariably wrongly connected, the stamps you were given were always the wrong ones, the tea you were offered was always coffee.

"Monsieur Van Dongen is not in, is he?"

"Yes, monsieur."

"Has he gone out?"

"No, monsieur."

"So he is in."

"Yes, he is not in, monsieur."

"How do you work with these people?" I asked the Austrian hotel manager. "We can't," he answered, "but we have to. The government is building schools all right, but they started too late and they don't teach in French. Besides, a boy who has completed primary school does not want to be a bellboy, he thinks he is a 'Herr Doktor.'"

They had started too late, particularly with the secondary and vocational schools and especially the universities. I was shown the Louvanium, the new private university, and its new medical school. The buildings on a hill commanding a grandiose view of Leo were still half finished, but a handful of African medical students were being prepared for service to their own people.

Only since 1954 had the government started to operate schools of its own; previously men of the cloth had done all the teaching in the Congo and it had been practically impossible for most Congolese to receive more than a primary education. In recent years many secondary and vocational schools of good quality had been set up by the government, and by 1957, 22,000 students were enrolled in competently staffed technical schools and workshops. But even then, in schools below the secondary level, the teaching language was still one of the many regional tongues, and hence people with primary schooling were still practically limited in French to *"Oui, monsieur."* Until after World War II only an infinitesimal percentage of girls had received any schooling at all.

In the last few years Congolese education had expanded rapidly and their medical services were perhaps the most advanced in all tropical Africa. The Congo Medical Service, with less than six hundred doctors, had worked wonders in this huge territory, two-thirds the size of the United States, where 13 million people were compressed into a few densely crowded cities (25 per cent) and scattered throughout an enormous near vacuum of savannah and virgin forest (75 per cent). Their progress in preventive medicine became spectacular after World War II. The endemic diseases, which had ravaged the entire continent throughout history, had here been curbed; yellow fever had ceased to be a menace, smallpox was practically eliminated. Sleeping sickness—except for cattle trypanosomiasis—was almost wiped out. Yaws, which produced the phantasmagorically mutilated faces of yesteryear, was under control and so was leprosy, thanks to the sulfones. The leprosaria, dreaded garbage cans of humanity, had been converted into neat villages where contagious cases could be treated and neutralized as fast as possible. Here the mutilated from before the sulfone period could be rehabilitated and the disabled taken care of. Only 10 per cent of 300,000 sufferers of leprosy now remained in these villages; the other 90 per cent were treated in their home villages and were co-operating eagerly with ambulatory teams from treatment centers. There were 3,500 of these treatment centers in 1958, mostly manned by specially trained African auxiliary personnel. Malaria had been eradicated in the large cities and treatment schemes were progressing in the rural areas.

Tuberculosis had been tackled with the new drugs on a national scale and the whole population was compulsorily X-rayed by mobile units once a year. I saw such a unit in action. It was near Mosango where a huge sanatarium had been built in a savannah country, which could only be reached by chartered plane and jeep. It seemed inconceivable that even before the independence riots this "model hospital" would be sacked by its own cowed patients. I had not liked Mosango with its silly bungalow luxury for the medical staff. Moreover, it was one of the few hospitals I saw in the Belgian Congo where the attitudes of the doctors were more those of policemen than of healers. I spoke to the technician on one of the X-ray trucks, a

primitive, hard-drinking white, who had taken this job after many failures in life and was prepared for it by a short course. He told me he was thirty-eight, but he looked like a man in his late fifties. His complexion was waxen and his lusterless eyes stood deep in fat folds of pale skin. "You'll see how those blacks behave in front of an X-ray machine, you'll laugh your head off! Some of them are so scared they stand on their heads or they wiggle and dance all the time." "But how can you take your pictures then?" I asked. "You just said you took an average of twelve hundred a day!" "Oh," the man said, "we got ourself two strong young blacks and they hold them against the screen." "You mean," I cried in horror, "that those two fellows get twelve hundred doses of X-ray a day?" "Well, what of it?" said the technician. "It is not that dangerous, is it? I get plenty of it myself."

But then, I visited hospitals where one Belgian doctor and a few nuns worked day and night in total self-forgetfulness. These nuns, strong peasant women who had never lived a woman's life and who, bright-eyed, slaved twenty hours a day without knowing they were slaving, still found time to plant Flemish gardens full of flowers, vegetables, and fruit trees in their forelorn savannah. They adopted the black mothers and their children as if they were their own brood. In their medieval garb, fluttering like white birds, rushing through the chiaroscuro of the tropical hospital, their Flemish peasant faces raw from the sun, they looked like fragments of a Memlinc painting lost in Africa.

I stayed for a few days in a leprosarium, where a young Belgian leprologist of unusual brilliance—he had been offered professorships all over the world—was succeeding in patiently building a community out of a dung heap. Meanwhile he had to fight every little step against old medical prejudices and bureaucratic rigidity. He also introduced rehabilitation, did valuable research on leprosy, and raised his patients to a new level of hope and dignity.

At the outpost of Bikoro I saw a neat hospital where other mild and energetic nuns were training Congolese nurses and where the Belgian district officer showed me, as if he were a proud father, the new houses he had helped his villagers to build. He pointed out the sewing machines and the furniture which he had inspired them to save for.

I met schoolteachers who could have stayed comfortably in Belgium, but who came here with burning idealism to help build up an educated human community. I knew territorial inspectors who wore the uniforms of colonial officials, but who loved their people, who knew the cultural anthropology of their regions inside out and profoundly respected the customs.

This was the new type of colonial civil servant, and as such

despised and obstructed by the thick-necked "colons" with their whisky-soaked wisdom. Given ten years more, they could have built in the Congo a human community which in education, health, and social security would have been an example for all of black Africa. But they did not get their chance. In January, 1959, barely three months after I had traveled through this land, where a smiling propaganda man had driven me along the new highways, pointing out the new buildings of Shell and Lever and General Motors, past neat new rows of white stucco houses for Africans, the first riots of Leopoldville occurred. Comparatively mild riots, they were incompetently handled, because no one in the colony had sufficient authority without having to check with the "management" in Brussels, who might of course be off for the weekend—as it happened during these first riots. The Belgians panicked and the colony started to disintegrate with incredible rapidity toward its inevitable doom.

How was this possible in a country so tightly organized, so perfectly and centrally ruled from Brussels? The answer lies in the hidden but basic disharmony behind the shiny façade. There was no official color bar, but in reality there was strict segregation in residential areas, in clubs, in jobs, and social contact. No black man had even risen to a position higher than clerk or noncommissioned officer. There was unemployment in the cities, full of unassimilated newcomers from the bush; there was poverty in the villages, only the mining areas and the rubber plantations prospered. Over all was the general irresistible surge of the "colonial peoples" which exploded throughout Asia and Africa and even across the Congo River in then French Equatorial Africa, to which President de Gaulle granted independence in 1958.

The Congo had been peremptorily ruled from board rooms and ministries in Brussels, as if it were the suburban branch of a bakery. There was neither time nor machinery to adapt to the new situation. Volumes have been filled with belated theories and explanations full of retrospective wisdom.

When I returned six months after the riots, the proud face of Leopoldville had fallen. Its spine was broken. New buildings remained unfinished, shops were empty. The boys at the Memlinc were sullen and hardly said even *"Oui, Monsieur."* In the fantastically colorful market I now got dirty glances and unkind words. Visual delights were blotted out by the tension in the heavy atmosphere. It was quiet, but it was the quiet of impending dissolution. The doctors, the teachers, the officials, all had lost their self-assurance and abandoned their ambitions. Even the arrogant immigration people seemed meek, and as soon as private conversation with any official started it turned immediately to "What shall I do when we are thrown out?" Served by sullen waiters, they sat on the terraces discussing whether it would end in five years, as King Baudouin thought, or in ten. Nobody, even in jest, believed it could be within months.

Nine months later a symbolical photograph of the Independence celebrations in Leopoldville appeared in the world press. It showed a smiling young white monarch being robbed of his sword by a gleeful Congolese prankster.

At the time of writing it looks as if chaos will take over the Congo for the foreseeable future. The teachers and doctors have fled. Overnight they had become hated foreigners in the new Congo Republic, without even consular or diplomatic protection, without any guarantee of safety or salary. The generally predicted strife between the tribal communities is raging and even the precarious peace of the world is once again threatened by the interference of the Eastern and Western powers.

Franck '18
Congo River

Mambo's Village

The Congo Republic (900,000 square miles) lies in the Congo basin which is a basin indeed. Its low-lying bottom of typical rain forest, marshes, and savannahs is surrounded by ridges which in the East rise to the 16,795 feet of the Ruwenzori Mountains.

Its population is nearly 14 million; Leopoldville, its capital, has 400,000 inhabitants, and Stanleyville 71,000. There is strong urbanization and detribalization of at least 25 per cent of the population.

About 4 million are Roman Catholic, about 1 million Protestant.

Its early inhabitants, the Pygmies, have been replaced through Bantu and Nilotic invasions. The first white contact was made by Portuguese navigators in the fifteenth century. Sir Henry Morton Stanley made his famous trip down the Congo in 1874 and was subsequently commissioned by Leopold II of Belgium to pursue his explorations and make treaties with tribal chiefs. In 1878 Leopold formed the International Association of the Congo and personally ruled the independent state of the Congo, recognized at the Berlin Conference in 1885–1886. Scandalous treatment of the Congolese in mines and on plantations resulted in the end of his personal rule in 1908, when Leopold transferred the Congo to the Belgian government as a colony.

After World War I, and especially during and after World War II, the Belgians so improved the social and economic conditions of the native population that the African standard of living in the Belgian Congo became higher than that of all the surrounding countries. Health and welfare were improved rapidly, and intensive local campaigns against endemic diseases were proving successful. Workman's compensation for occupational diseases and accidents had been enforced since 1949.

In 1952 systematic plans for better housing were put into effect. Where the Belgians failed perhaps most spectacularly was in the field of education, as well as in the furtherance of African participation in local politics. The Congo was ruled from Brussels, and civil rights were granted to neither the Congolese nor the European settlers in the Congo. From 1948 to 1958 the number of children attending schools had doubled in the rural areas and quadrupled in the urban areas. Vocational and trade schools increased their numbers tenfold during the last ten years of Belgian rule. Institutions of higher learning were founded in 1956, and at the time of Independence, June 30, 1960, the Louvanium University near Leopoldville was ready to graduate its first medical students.

Congo political consciousness seems not to have sprung up until 1956, when the first political association of Congolese was formed. Since then, hundreds of political parties have appeared, mostly based on local or tribal groupings. Patrice Lumumba's National Congolese Movement, although built on the tribal loyalties of the Oriental Province, was the first party with a semblance of national following. Ever since independence the new state has been plagued by problems caused by tribal antagonisms and the personal ambitions of its politicians. At the time of writing, anarchy, tribal warfare, economic breakdown, organizational confusion, and the precarious UN intervention are undoing the even modest beginnings of economic security and threaten to involve Africa as well as the world in war.

In 1960 three-quarters of the population of the Congo were still living from subsistence agriculture, moving their cultures of manioc, corn, yams, and some cotton from exhausted plot to plot. Land tenure, which traditionally was tribal and collective, had just begun to be made individual by the Belgians in order to try and increase productivity. Agricultural settlements, started by the colonial power in order to be distributed to indigenous family groups, were outfitted with medical centers, schools, and co-operatives. Twenty-five per cent of the population had migrated to cities and industrial centers. Consumer goods were being imported and produced, but the demand for them outstripped the supply as African purchasing power increased. During the last ten years of Belgian rule foreign trade quadrupled, with a favorable export balance for the Congo, resulting in a spectacular increase in living standards. The principal capital investment, almost entirely Belgian-owned, was in mining and steel, which contributed more than one-third of the annual revenues. The principal exports in 1958 were cotton, coffee, palm oil, copper, diamonds, cobalt, and uranium.

mahogany lumbering near Lambarene

Franck '58

10 / Lambaréné Revisited

The sky between Lagos and Douala reflected the turbulence in the Cameroons. It had been placid above Western Nigeria, but by the time the old DC-3 tried to cross Eastern Nigeria, it was tossed about like a feather by black thunderclouds. Lightning enveloped the plane, intent on destroying it, and I was most surprised to arrive at all. In Douala a few soldiers with fixed bayonets were standing around the murky airfield. Last year I had not known anything about the terrorism which in the past twelve months had taken six hundred lives. When the customs officer had asked me solemnly, "Have you any arms?" I had joked, "*Seulement un petit canon.*" The man had glanced at me and his look said plainly, "Idiot!"

Now a porter, with deep tribal carvings on his face, was carrying my bags to a little bus marked "Hotel des Cocotiers." He did not thank me for my tip. A few dusty soldiers with bayonets opened the barbed wire entanglements before the control tower building. "*Comment ça va maintenant ici?*" I asked the driver, but I got no answer. People in Douala have learned not to answer questions.

The bus drove quickly the half mile to the Hotel des Cocotiers and we met only a jeepful of armed soldiers. The hotel is modern luxurious, and was nearly empty, yet I was given a room on the fifth floor. "It is much quieter this year," the manager told me. "This week only three people were killed—that customs

151

officer at M'Ongo who was hacked to pieces, and Father Courtecuisse who was shot down on his way to Mass, and some terrorist, apparently, who had Czech ammunition and Communist literature in his house."

The dining room on the top floor, elegant and large as that of a luxury hotel on the Riviera, was empty. Red-jacketed African waiters were yawning. In the far corner a man whom I had seen on the plane was frowning over the menu. The phonograph, playing syncopated Bach furiously, emphasized the already frightening silence. The lone man shouted desperately in an American accent: "Anybody speak English around here?" "Can I help you?" I called over to him. "I can't make head or tail of this," he said, waving the menu at me and coming over. "I want a steak or something, my wife is sick upstairs," the man said, and started to describe the unappetizing symptoms of amoebic dysentery. He was a thin, puritanical-looking provincial. "Are you a missionary?" I asked. "Hell, no." He grinned. "We are Terre Haute, you see, I just retired so we are taking this trip. We always wanted to; but, gee is this a scary place! What is it called anyway?" He pulled an itinerary out of his pocket, marked "Atlas Travel Agency, Terre Haute. . . . We get you there."

Outside my window the palm leaves—I had never before been on the same level with the top of a palm tree—were hanging motionless. The grounds were floodlit all night, and a soldier, rifle in hand, paced up and down at the edge of the half-finished blue and yellow mosaic swimming pool. Beyond him the jungle stretched gray in the moonlight, and a luminous surf was breaking on the beach.

It was pleasant to leave Douala and fly through an overcast sky to the Gabon Republic. In the plane I set next to a gray-haired African with a finely cut face, who was correcting a manuscript. He addressed me in especially elegant French. "Are you going to visit our newly independent country?" he asked, slightly ironically, "in which case I bet you are going to Dr. Schweitzer." He was the editor of a local newspaper, a patriot and a conservative, which made him a friend of Mr. Leon M'Ba, Prime Minister of the new republic. "During the independence celebrations," the editor told me, "M'Ba made a speech which was a model of moderation. He was educated in France like myself, and for years he was a deputy in the French Parliament. The Premier sees very well that the Gabon needs France. As long as Mr. M'Ba is premier here, the Gabon will be a cultivated country, but," he added with a worried look, "elections are coming, and if the demagogues win we might get into a Congo-like situation. Then I would not vouch for the safety of your friend Schweitzer either."

"What do you think of Schweitzer?" I asked. "Oh, I admire the man," he replied, "I realize very well that without Schweitzer few people would ever have heard about our country. He has done tremendous good here. But the young hotheads hate him and that is understandable too, for they can't realize that Schweitzer has been here for nearly fifty years and that when I was a child he was about the only doctor in the whole country. They only see that there are now modern hospitals here and there and that the Schweitzer hospital is becoming an antique."

At the Libreville airport *buvette* they were drinking beer. The blond woman behind the counter was shouting instructions to the kitchen. A black boy, shining like a new shoe, brought in a large *capitaine* fish for Friday lunch.

The next stop was Port Gentil. The customs officer with his heavy, kind black face recognized me. He had been my patient at Lambaréné last year and asked me for a prescription for pills to improve his potency. At the mouth of the Ogowe River lies Port Gentil—an enormous sky of pearly gray, a strip of beach

with a few high palms, a sleepy street parallel to the beach with new ugly houses built by the Petroleum Company. There is not a ripple on the polished mirror of the bay. Not a soul stirs in the Sunday streets except one man in a battered felt Homburg, who walks his dog. He looks as if he were walking in Valenciennes and had forgotten to put on his winter coat.

Here in the air-conditioned, gleaming new hotel I waited for my plane connection to Lambaréné. Since the country has become independent it has its own airline, which consists only of a few planes chartered from Air France and hence the number of flights has been greatly reduced. But to rest two days in this pleasant atmosphere of indolence is no punishment. Main Street has a few bookshops with the newest French literature. Is this turbulent Africa? All the Africans speak French, and waiters and postal workers talk to you like equals, quite naturally and with dignity. How far away is humming Lagos, terrorist-infested Douala, and seething ex-Belgian Congo? *Ici tout est calme et beauté.* . . .

Lambaréné from the air: a homecoming. The plane again noses its way over the green jungle soup with its patches of island and comes down on the airstrip, where they are now building a smart control tower. At the Ogowe River ferry, the large pirogue from the hospital is waiting and the rowers Emile and Obiange and *petit* Jean welcome me like a lost brother. The river is very low in the middle of the dry season and on the large sand flats fishermen are camping in palm-leaf huts. Little black boys are playing a game, sliding off the high river banks into the turbid water. The same crews on the same old steamers are still coming and going and we recognize each other. A boy in a pirogue shouts, *"Bonjour, Docteur!"*

At the hospital landing there are more pirogues than ever. Dr. Schweitzer has aged. He is building again, a row of new huts for his workers near the new garage. He looks worried and drawn, completely wrapped up in his building. "I still have to build this," he says. "When I am dead they can get on for a few years yet, but then there will be nobody here who can organize this." It was the first time I had heard him mention anything about the hospital after his death. I am constantly asked about Dr. Schweitzer's plans for his hospital and usually answer: "Can you predict what will happen in Africa next week? How can anyone make plans?"

The hospital has not changed. There are two new doctors and a few new monkeys. The young pelican has become an adult and a tame member of the family, and the velvety litter of off-

white kittens of last year is now a family of mangy cats. Main Street is still choked with the sick, the shouts of *"Brancardier, brancardier!"* still sound from the beach when new emergencies arrive in canoes. I think I hear a woman singing from a pirogue midstream. The pirogue comes closer and what I thought was a song is a heart-rending wail. As the pirogue touches the beach the woman jumps out holding a child in her arms. The child's head dangles passively as the mother runs on her thin strong legs to the hospital.

Yet, also in Lambaréné things change. In the Leper Village a radio blares; it was given by a visitor. First I hear music, then a demagogue from Leopoldville speaks. Something has changed in the mood here too, and since Nurse Trudy left the children have forgotten their songs.

The old man was sitting at his table, writing. His head, bent low over his note paper, nearly rested on the table. He muttered something, started to rummage in his papers, could not find what he was looking for, and muttered louder. His housekeeper-nurse-secretary, Mathilde, must have heard him, for she appeared

in the doorway looking at the mess on the desk. Her hands folded she asked softly, "Were you looking for something, *Docteur?*" "Did I call you? Then stay where you are," growled the old man. Mathilde left meekly and Schweitzer went on digging in his papers. Then he got up, angrily. The old massive torso bent, the legs a bit curved in the frayed khaki trousers, the square bushy head thrust forward. He started to leaf through the clusters of clippings, bundled together with string, hanging from nails behind his desk. He was still mumbling, found what he wanted, and lowered himself onto the hard square stool ("I don't like chairs, I despise comfort"). He licked his fingers and leafed through the file of clippings.

Then he started to write again. His face was even closer to the paper now, a face built around a central massif core; the large pitted nose as its base and the heavy brow-arch as its top. From it radiated innumerable lines deepening into grooves which divided the aged flesh into planes; above his glasses the bushy eyebrows were knitting and unknitting, hairs sprouting and jumping over the rims. The line of the eyebrows was repeated two or three times in parallel grooves on his forehead. The skin looked hard, old, and element-beaten. The white mustache bristled over his mouth and nearly caressed the paper.

The old strong hand slowly, deliberately wrote on. Then after a sentence or two his head would straighten and turn. For a few seconds it would be fixed toward the glassless window with its mosquito screening and look out over the river. Suddenly he seemed to notice me again. "Shall I pose for you?" he asked kindly. "Oh, no, please go on working, I'll sketch while you work." "Yes, but not with my glasses," he said, "they make me look too old." Within a minute he had forgotten me and was writing again. It was getting dark and the cicada music had become as strong and irritating as a blaring radio. The file of ants marching across his table got out of focus in the growing dusk.

When he pulled the oil lamp toward him and lighted it, I noticed for the first time that he was wearing cotton sleevelets over his wrists so that the sweat would not soil his paper. After a few more sentences he got up again. He took the sleevelets off and put on a faded crumpled felt hat. "Let's sit down outside," he said.

I followed him out of the room and we sat on the steps of his porch, looking at the dusk deepening over the river. He seemed sad about something he had just read. "One should have the skin of a hippo," he said abruptly and without explanation, "and the soul of an angel." His dog Tshutshu sat between us. Mathilde came noiselessly behind us, standing erect with the toucan Jackie on her shoulder, who was peering at us from the beads on both sides of his ludicrous beak.

The old man looked at the evening and absorbed it. "Look at that tree," he said, pointing at a kapok in the distance. It still was caressed by the last light of day. We stayed, silent, a few minutes longer. The darkness had fallen quickly like a hood over the landscape. The dinner gong was sounding and kerosene lanterns started their dance to the dining room. "*Ja, ja,*" sighed the old man. He got up heavily, took his kerosene lamp from the shelf, and we all crossed the yard to the dining room. We put our burning lamps to wait for us in the little hall.

The twenty people in the dining room, who had been talking, became quiet and sat down. The last chair stopped scraping on the concrete floor. Schweitzer's eyes quickly darted up and down the long table, then they closed.

"Thank the Lord, for He is kind and His goodness is everlasting. Amen," he said quietly.

During dinner I told him about a class of a public school in a poor section of the Bronx, where I had given a talk some time

ago. The children, all thirty of them, had written letters to Dr. Schweitzer. "I just thanked them in your name," I said, "I guess that is all right." But the old doctor wanted to know all about it and when I read to him some of the names—Spanish, Italian, Jewish, Polish, Chinese—and told him about the teacher who made it her task to teach all these white, pink, yellow, and black children to get on together, he looked at me with suddenly very young eyes under the bushy white eyebrows. "But this is important," he cried, "this is really important."

After dinner he asked me to his room and I watched him write with his old hands slowly and steadily two letters, one to the children of P.S. 53 in the Bronx and one to the teacher:

. . . I myself come from an old Alsatian family of schoolmasters. My grandfather, his four brothers and two sisters were schoolmasters. And I, deep down in my heart, am a schoolmaster and have a schoolmaster's soul. That is why I understand so well your work in the difficult and very special profession of a teacher. . . .

He is more than a great man, I thought, he is a great human being.

While I was drawing next day, an African joined me. He was fortyish, thin and intense. It was clear he wanted to ask me for something. It was money. Then he started to complain bitterly about the hospital. He said he was working on the new road and hardly got paid. "Just because my wife is sick, I have to work like a slave," he snarled. "And the *Grand Docteur* insults us when he gets mad at us. You don't do that any more to us blacks. If he were a younger man, I'd bash his head in."

Even Lambaréné is changing. The "winds of change" which sweep all over Africa are not stopped by any wall of mahogany and okoumé trees. Schweitzer is still the great witch doctor to the old, but the young *évolués* dislike the hospital. It may have

162

been true twenty years ago that the Africans were afraid of a gleaming white hospital and preferred one which reminded them of their villages. Schweitzer has often said so and his hospital did become a cross between an Alsatian farm and a native African village.

But the young Africans have a new god. Not the Christian one, whom they never really accepted—Christianity is losing in Africa, Islam is gaining—but the cruel god Progress. In Lagos I saw Yoruba women who lived in slums without plumbing or any sanitation proudly push the buttons of the self-service elevator in their new skyscraper hospital. No condescending pseudo-villages for them, but the shiny gadgets, the roaring power of

car, plane, bus, and tractor, which at last will make them equals of the whites.

"Why is there no sanitary water in that hospital?" the bus driver asked me, blinking through his sunglasses. His hands were behind his khaki back and his chin was thrust up aggressively. He is the man who drives his bus from Lambaréné to Libreville and back once a week. "Why didn't the Grand Docteur ever start a school to train black nurses? Why are there still those dirty old bunks and no beds? Why does he separate the Fang and the Galwa patients? That was O.K. fifty years ago, but we are all Gabonais now, aren't we? Come on, *Docteur,* have

you ever seen the hospital at Libreville?" The bus driver knows what he is talking about. The hospital at Libreville, five hours by bus, is hypermodern and built in the latest international style. It is huge and no doubt excellent. "All of Gabon has only about fifty doctors, and look how this old hospital is filled day after day with three hundred and fifty patients or more," I answer. "How can you doubt it is useful?"

But the chauffeur is the New Africa, and his quarrel with the Lambaréné hospital is not based on reason but on emotion. "*C'est dégoutant,*" he repeats. And he will repeat it at all the bus stops between Lambaréné and Libreville.

On this third trip to Lambaréné my heart grew heavier and heavier. In America Schweitzer is criticized because the press took hold of him and exploited this news item until it became an irritant. His imbecilic adorers still pretend that his hospital is the only hospital in Africa, the only medical center on the tropical continent to which all the little Africans come running to have their ulcers cured with potassium permanganate; as if there were no hospitals and doctors all over Africa, albeit too few; as if there were no World Health Organization. Hysterical females sing his praise in falsetto and pour their adulation over women's club audiences, making a career out of eulogizing the old doctor, until those who never did anything creative in their lives feel justified in dismissing this great human being as a phony.

Meanwhile the old man plods on. Somewhere deep inside he must know that, although he was the pioneer of medical help in Equatorial Africa, he has been overtaken. He must, with his probing intelligence and his real love of human beings, feel deeply unhappy that he has underestimated the Africans surrounding him. But even there I defend him, and have defended him against attacks all over the West Coast of Africa. For all the African doctors and intellectuals attacked me on Schweitzer, whom they see as a vestige of colonialism, paternalism, and a Christian endeavor they don't understand and hence despise. "He may be the noblest flower of colonialism, he is typical of the era," they say. They seem to decry the old curative hospital, which even if it is not modern and not perfect, has relieved suf-fering for nearly half a century. They think only in terms of the mass approach of preventive medicine. Meanwhile many African doctors, who are so quick to criticize the old pioneer, them-selves flock to the cities, where almost all of them work for status, money, large houses, and gleaming cars.

Schweitzer has never been in Africa, I have often argued. After his short European "vacations," during which he gave talks or organ concerts to raise money for his hospital, he took the boat from Bordeaux to Port Gentil and from there the slow *pinasse* to Lambaréné, where he buried himself in work among a poverty-ridden, backward agricultural people. The more devel-oped countries of West Africa he has never seen, and who of us a few years ago knew what went on in Accra, Abidjan, Lomé, or Yaounde? Who knows now? Meanwhile the Grand Docteur worked and cured and wrote and played his piano-organ and the years flew by, and the inroads of education and culture in his poverty-stricken district were far from spectacular. If he had come from his native Alsace to some forlorn hillbilly village in the Ozarks and never left it except by air, would he have a high estimate of American culture from direct observation?

My intellectual African friends often understood this argument, but my anxiety remained. If there were only hope of modernizing Lambaréné in time! But how can we expect Dr. Schweitzer at eighty-six to adapt himself to the mutations of Africa? Even if he were to install electricity and water and a school for nurses—even if he were to streamline his hospital out of recognition, banish his animals into kraals, import African

doctors (from where?), who would guarantee that it would be sufficient?

One day Schweitzer must die, and the loss of this great human soul, this gigantic example of what a man can do with his life, will leave us all much poorer.

He asked me with something at once hopeful and hopeless in his eyes, "Do you believe that the idea of Reverence for Life is gaining ground?" Reverence for Life. . . . I came from New York and had traveled all over exploding West Africa, across half of a globe which seemed to be getting ready to destroy itself in a last general spasm of insane violence. Timidly I said, "I don't know. There has never been so much violence. And yet, you sowed a seed. . . ."

We were standing at the bend of the new road Schweitzer is

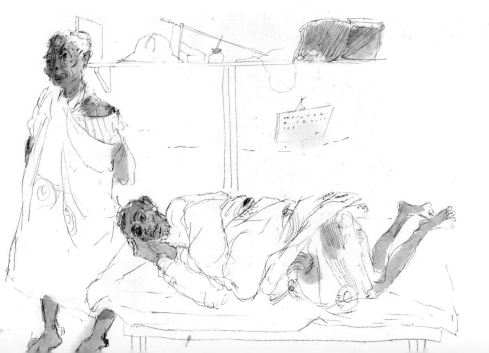

building. After forty-seven years he has given in: the hospital will be accessible by car and truck instead of by canoe only. A yellow bulldozer was flattening the underbrush and the African driver was singing. The old man bent down stiffly and lifted a few much too heavy rocks. He put them carefully by the side of the road and mumbled: "I can use them for building later."

Virtually the entire territory of the Gabon Republic (103,000 square miles) is situated in the basin of the Ogowe River, which is more than 500 miles long and is to a great extent navigable. Its vegetation is rapid and dense and, seen from the air, the whole area seems to be entirely covered by rain forest.

The population is composed of about 400,000 Africans and less than 5,000 Europeans. More than 90 per cent live in the rural areas. The capital, Libreville, has 21,000 inhabitants.

There is a small remnant of the original Pygmy inhabitants. Bantus live in the Delta region and along the lower Ogowe River. The latest arrivals are the Fangs, a tribe which infiltrated from the North in the nineteenth century.

There are few Christians; most of the population are animists.

The country was discovered by the Portuguese in the fifteenth century, and their trading posts and missions at the mouth of the Ogowe River date from that period. English, Dutch, and French followed, and religion and slave-trading were actively pursued by the French. Since the beginning of the nineteenth century, when the coastal ports were occupied by the French, the slave trade has been prohibited. Libreville was founded in 1849 as a city for freed slaves.

In 1890 Gabon became part of the French Congo, but in 1910 it was organized as a separate colony and in 1958 it became an autonomous republic in the French Community. Its Prime Minister, Leon M'Ba, is a member of the Executive Council of the Community. The Parliamentary Democracy of the Gabon was created in 1959. At present all political parties agree that a direct federation with France is more advantageous to the young republic than federation with the other French Equatorial African republics.

Per capita income in 1958 was about $55 a year. Cocoa is the important export crop. Other exports are lumber, mahogany and okoume, but deforestation is an imminent threat. Potentially there is great mineral wealth. Iron, discovered in 1895, was not exploited until 1955, and operations in the richest iron fields have not yet started, chiefly because of transportation difficulties. A beginning oil production raises hope also of increased prosperity.

Health is notoriously poor and infant mortality high. Leprosy, malaria, tuberculosis, and yaws are common. There is increased public eagerness for medical care, and modern hospitals exist in Libreville and Port Gentil. However, there are only fifty doctors active in the entire Gabon Republic.

11 / Garden Party
at Lastourville

The Lambaréné airstrip is no Idlewild. Every time a plane circles, you know it is *the* plane. Dark heads everywhere lift toward the sky as for the Second Coming. In the Land Rover we bobbed along the dirt road, waved at from the huts, and arrived at the airstrip. What looked like a hundred people, mostly Africans, were waiting for the plane: men in their Sunday best in orange trousers and yellow silk shirts; women in crazy-quilt wraps, their children on their backs; dignified black officials with their untutored wives ("*Vous êtes avec une femme ou avec deux?*" the steward asked), and crowds of big-eyed children. Two particularly elegant specimens in rumpled jackets—one with a Hawaiian sport shirt underneath, another in a jaunty racing cap—stood a little apart from the crowd.

After a short time we all scrambled into the old DC-4—the ingredients for a fine and brotherly jelly if a few screws got loose! The captain walked through the cabin, a thin somewhat bent and unhappy looking fellow of about forty-five with a small mustache and eyes which looked disgusted and also a little yellow. I remember thinking, "gastric ulcer, bad liver." He paced all the way down the cabin and said angrily to the steward, "Get them all up front, can't you see we are overweight? Our point of gravity is much too far to the back." All the people behind me were somehow pushed beyond the door which divided the fuselage in two; whether they were sitting,

lying, or hanging I'll never know, for although the door flew open every minute, it was kicked closed again too quickly to see what was going on behind it.

We were flying already and there was the river, the Schweitzer Hospital, and the god-awful jungle, stretching endlessly; the stink, the heat, and the anxiety were almost unbearable. There would be three stops before Brazzaville. At the first stop some Africans got off to go to their villages and a few white passengers joined us. The second stop would be Lastourville. The plane touched down and made a sort of jolly jump on what is called a runway in this part of the world. We piled out as the chickens and goats scattered before the invasion from outer space. The dinner-jacketed gentlemen and their wives and many others clambered into a truck which served as the local limousine service. The other passengers walked out of the sun to spend the half hour for loading and unloading in the shade of one of the three small buildings which formed the only shelter on the airstrip. The main building was about twenty feet long and one story high, with four glassless windows and no door. On it in faded lettering was painted: "Lastourville." Two smaller sheds carried respectively the words "Méteo" and "T.S.F."

We sat in "Méteo," because there were a few chairs and a bed. A few minutes later Madame "Méteo," very pretty and

young, walked in with a child at her breast. She sat down to complete the feeding, smiling at us. Only then I noticed that this was not a waiting room, but the bed-sitting-drawing room of Mr. and Mrs. "Méteo." Mr. "Méteo" also came in soon, sat down, and said, "Well, you'll have a long time here."—"More than half an hour?" I asked. "Ah, *oui, monsieur,*" he said, "maybe tomorrow"—he had the beautiful ivory smile of Africa —and went on, "I have just radioed to Brazza." "But what's happened?" I asked bewildered. "Something wrong?" "But didn't you notice? You smashed two wheels of your landing gear coming down."

I went out and saw indeed that there were more people standing around and under the plane than usual; for on an African airstrip there are always a number of unauthorized visitors watching the proceedings of fueling, loading, and unloading, a few of them with lighted cigarettes in their mouths. There was very little left of two of our three wheels and the jolly little jump at the landing might well have been our last one.

The answer that came back from Brazza obviously said that it was Sunday and *"que voulez-vous? . . . C'est la période des vacances."* But tomorrow morning they would send a plane to pick us up. Nobody was excited. The eighteen passengers merely shrugged their shoulders, and the captain found a bottle of whisky. We sat in our dead plane, waiting for the flight engineer to come back from his explorations in the town of Lastourville, about five miles away.

After a while I went for a walk down the road to look at the few mud huts. Before the first one a woman sat on her haunches, a bronze statue; she looked at me impassively. In front of the second hut an old woman, her breasts bare, was delousing her daughter. The third hut bore a sign with a name and under it, "*Ancien combattant* 1914–1918." An old man in yellow trousers, the remains of an army tunic, and a faded scarlet fatigue cap on his gray curls, arose from a box in his bone-dry dirt front yard and saluted gravely. His neighbors, one in a nightshirt, the other in old blue shorts, grinned and we exchanged a few words in French. In the trembling heat we must have been apparitions to each other.

Back at the plane my fellow passengers were still drinking whisky. It was stifling. I sat down and read an old *Paris-Match*. The captain looked a little less grim after his third whisky. "Do we sleep in the plane?" I asked him. "Maybe," he said. "We have two DDT bombs," the steward consoled us pleasantly. "I know," I said, because they had fallen on me during the jump. There was the sound of a jeep in the distance and the navigator came back. He had a bottle in his hand, "with the compliments of the Commissaire de District," who was also trying to arrange lodgings for us for the night. But it was difficult, for Lastourville only had four European families. There was plenty of space for the African passengers, however.

Another truck arrived and we were taken to the heart of the village. The road went downhill, past the huts I had already seen, and kept on going downhill for five hundred feet, through a dark funnel of dense virgin forest. Then all at once we were at the end of the funnel: a vast valley spread out below, with the wide Ogowe River winding through it and rows of mountains receding into a blue background behind it, as in a medieval painting. Deep down in this Shangri-La a few neat houses formed a circle; in front of the biggest one were two flagpoles with the French and Gabon flags flying in a lazy wind. We drove through a little Arc de Triomphe of trained trees and in the open doorway of the white, flower-bedecked bungalow stood the Commissaire de District. He was a fat man, smiling happily; he had a pipe in his mouth, and a slightly wry neck on high shoulders gave him a quite aristocratic appearance. He wore a dark green sweater and said simply, "*Soyez les bienvenus,*" adding, "won't you join me in a drink on the terrace?" as if this had been a carefully arranged garden party to which he had been looking forward. His servants noiselessly passed whisky, crème de menthe, and champagne. Three immense palm trees had their roots deep under the terrace, from which one could see the blue-green vegetation going down steeply a few hundred yards to the river's rocky edge. Below, the river was calm and a pirogue drifted dreamily toward the distant wild rapids. A little farther downstream the waters divided to embrace a high island, a patch of virgin forest which must have swarmed with a complete collection of African fauna. My eye followed the river to the bend, where it disappeared in a horizon of golden haze.

On the terrace twelve people, who had yesterday never suspected each other's existence, were drinking champagne together in a fantasy which had lost all contact with reality. The conversation was general and forced. Only the Commissaire de District belonged here and he found it so commonplace that he did not even show off his house, which was open on all sides to the coming evening.

Next to me sat a French-speaking American missionary, who had nothing to say. On my other side was a Texaco dealer from deep in the *brousse,* who looked like a French Gary Cooper. He felt obliged to throw a few words of broken English in my

direction once in a while. A surly, tall Commissaire de District from somewhere, was mainly interested in the gun collection of his colleague. A garage owner from Brazzaville told us the gruesome details of the intertribal riots: how at the roadblocks passers-by were simply asked: "What tribe?" and if the answer happened to be wrong, they were quickly decapitated. He described with relish how pregnant women were cleanly disemboweled. The young director of a new radio station and his tired-looking wife concentrated on their cherublike baby for whom the whole adventure did not yet exist. A lumberjack with a lean medieval face spoke in a very strong French patois and made jerky wooden gestures. The captain of the plane had put on a leather jacket and kept silent. An African journalist in a blue serge suit was talking softly with a French Jesuit missionary who looked like Jean Gabin.

Our host tried to entertain us with topics which in his opinion would interest everybody, mainly hunting stories and particulars about the African customs of his region. But the animals interested him more. On his walls were beautifully framed pages from Buffon's *Histoire naturelle,* and most of the books on his shelves were about animals. "Animals are my passion," he said as he got up, lightly for such a heavy man, and waved us to the buffet which had been prepared.

And here, hundreds of miles away from the next settlement,

in a funnel of virgin forest, on a large mahogany table covered with damask, waited an exquisite *buffet froid.* "You were unexpected, and I am sorry but you will just have to take potluck," smiled the Commissaire, waving his arm toward *caviar Mallosol, paté de campagne, foie gras, thon à la portugaise,* and thick slices of cold roast beef. There were freshly fried potato chips and many more complicated and tasteful things and warm fresh French bread. There was an endless supply of mellow Bordeaux and a particularly fruity, cool Moselle wine.

Had the plane really miraculously made so safe a landing? Or had we already ascended to some afterlife, standing around a table, piling plates with delicacies in front of wide open doors,

with the soft murmur of cataracts below and a too esthetic crescent moon over the palm trees?

After supper we returned to the terrace, and more drinks were served. In the stillness of the equatorial evening we were all enveloped in irreality.

"How long shall we still be tolerated on this continent?" mused the priest, sipping his cognac. "I don't know," said the Commissaire, "but I wouldn't know what to do in France, that I can tell you." "They'll still need us for a long time to come," growled the Texaco dealer. "They aren't reasonable enough to see that," said the radio man. "Their leaders know that they couldn't operate a radio station, that they couldn't drill the oil wells, that they haven't one single economist. But the young hotheads think they can do everything, because they are completely ignorant, and the Russians will try to confirm them in their beliefs and take over."

"We don't want to exchange a mild tyranny for a harsh one," said the African journalist. "We know very well that we got an education from you, that without your engineers, technicians, and doctors we are sunk. We need you administratively, medically, technically. But then, I am a moderate and I know it."

"Yes," said the Texaco man, "you know it. But still you want your 'independence,' don't you? And expect us to pay for everything, fill the gaps in your budget, defend you, and give you every service for free. Do you think that can go on forever? What is your press doing to make it clear to your people how much you need us? If we get out, you'll go back to the jungle in a few years' time. Look at the Congo," he said triumphantly, "I am told that Leopoldville is already beginning to be overgrown with jungle." "You'll start eating each other again," the lumberjack joined in viciously.

"I think we won't," said the journalist quietly. "We know it

will be difficult, but we have men of good will. We are divided in tribes and we cannot sweep away the old customs. But we have more than we ever had. We have French as a common language, we can communicate with each other. We want a civilized way of life, even the village people want it. Maybe they don't quite know yet what efforts it will demand of them." "And your politicians won't tell them either," said the pilot, mixing in for the first time. "They are just fighting about who will get the greatest power, the biggest car, and the most trips to Paris or the United Nations."

"They will learn. And our people will learn to distinguish between them," the journalist replied. "Our people are tired of being black sub-proletarians. They feel the need to live like other human beings. You have taught them that need, if you have taught them anything." "We may have taught you many needs," said the priest. "Maybe you were better off before we came. We have taught some of you in order to make you clerks in our offices and mechanics for our caterpillars. But we have failed to raise the level of the family, for how few girls have we trained? It is true, your people haven't co-operated very much.

. . . Now you want bicycles, radios, and sewing machines and cameras, and you think that is culture. And I'm afraid you'll sell your soul to whoever promises 'things' to you."

"You are thinking of the Russians again, *mon Père,*" said the journalist with a smile. "I grant you that where there are frustrated, discontented politicians and poverty-stricken populations the Communists have their chance. But we don't want them. The Chinese Communists have done fantastic things in the few years they have been in power, but we don't think their example could possibly work in tropical Africa. On the other hand, I grant you that we want the things you have. We want housing, food, hospitals, and education, especially education. But above all we want human dignity. You never gave us that, did you? You took it from us. You didn't mind doing things for us. But never with us. You despised us really. Now we want to build our countries ourselves, for we have learned that we are human beings like you. If anything, more human than you."

For a few moments nobody spoke. Then the priest said, "What I worry about is that you have no tradition of responsibility except to your clans, you have no tradition of the brotherhood of man except within your tribe, and we have not been able to instill it in you."

The African smiled again. "Aren't you a bit optimistic about the honesty of your own politicians? And your European history, as I read it, is not exactly a demonstration of brotherhood between *your* tribes."

"If you ask me," said the doctor, who had previously remained silent, "we are all in a mess. I love this country and I get on splendidly with the people. But very soon you'll throw me out. I think the tragedy is that there is not an evolution, a slow movement toward real autonomy, but just this disease of 'independence.' And you Africans grab for that as a child grabs for

the moon. I don't believe you people are inferior to us, I won't even believe you are so different. I think you have magnificent qualities, extraordinary vitality, great potentialities. But I feel that all Africa has been infected by a virus which we have brought you: nationalism. And this virus has driven you mad, it has given you delusions of grandeur and the belief that through a new magic you can stamp your foot and conjure up a society which can equal the old European society. But European society was not built in one day; it was based on long traditions of thrift, husbandry, investment, and inventiveness."

The journalist opened his mouth as if to speak, closed it again, and shrugged his shoulders. There was a strange cry from below. The Commissaire got up and nodded to me. He took his flashlight and some fruit from the table and I followed him below the terrace. A large baboon sat there on his scarlet buttocks and started to run excitedly in the circle allowed him by his leash. The Commissaire talked to him and the baboon sat down again, his large round eyes focused on his friend, who gave him a banana.

"You can talk about Africa until you are blue in the face," he sighed. "There is no such place as Africa. There is no common ground between the peoples of the Congo, Ethiopia, and Sierra Leone. There are hundreds of languages in every administrative unit. There are differences of soil, of climate, of religion, of customs. All it has in common are dark-skinned people with curly hair and protruding lips and the terrible infection called 'independence,' as the doctor says."

"Maybe there are some other things they have in common," I said. "They are not created equal, as little as we whites are created equal, although I believe absolutely that all of us—black, white, yellow, and green—are created equivalent: of equal human value. I agree with the journalist that Africans have

in common a sudden realization that they are men, and they long for human dignity. And with it comes the absolute resolve to share in the resources of their countries, and to share fairly. And a hope to better themselves. Their self-confidence is confirmed every day by those kinsmen who have reached positions of prominence and power in the world." "Assuming that you are right," said the Commissaire, "what will it mean to us?"

"Nothing easy," I replied. "We shall have to accept that all we have ever injected into Africa will be transformed beyond recognition, whether it is Christianity or democracy or perhaps even medicine. They will make it African and it will be different, compounded of old and new, theirs and ours. Not a mixture of both heritages, but a new compound. If this new product frightens us and we cannot accept it, we shall lose the continent spiritually, politically, and economically, and it will seal our doom, for Africa is awake now."

My host was petting his friend the baboon. The moon had disappeared and a hot, heavy breeze was blowing. On the terrace the guests dozed over their drinks. . . .

"Is Africa really awake?" the Commissaire said, pouring himself a last cognac, "or do we whites just think so because we are fast falling asleep?" He looked at me with a bitter smile and lifted his glass.

"Happy dreams, *mon ami!*"